Does a lack of self-confidence, or conversely, too much pride, keep you from realizing your life's dreams and goals? Do you find yourself a slave to the things of this world? Do you long for happiness in your personal relationships, for advancement in your career?

Dale Galloway shares 19 key principles for true success. He exhorts: "If you long to stand out, to be a winner in the game of life, then this book is for you!"

The life-changing principles taught here include:

- *The Achiever's Principle*
- *The Leadership Principle*
- *The Harvest Principle*
- *The Victory Principle*
- *The VIP Principle*

Within these pages, you will discover how to banish the fears that keep you from being all that God intended you to be.

Do you want to be your best to the glory of God? Let *Confidence Without Conceit* show you how!

CONFIDENCE
Without Conceit

BY Dale Galloway:

Dare to Discipline Yourself

Confidence Without Conceit

CONFIDENCE
Without Conceit

Dale E. Galloway

Power Books

Fleming H. Revell
Old Tappan, New Jersey

Library of Congress Cataloging-in-Publication Data

Galloway, Dale E.
    Confidence without conceit / Dale E. Galloway.
      p.   cm.
    ISBN 0-8007-5288-0
    1. Success—Religious aspects—Christianity. I. Title.
    BV4509.5.G35 1989
248.4—dc19   88-30193
                                                   CIP

Contents

Introduction

Without confidence you are like a 747 without fuel: You are masterfully designed to soar to the heights, yet without confidence, you are unable to go anywhere.

What happens to a person who lacks confidence? He wanders around in a wasteland of confusion, feeling like a nobody. Without confidence, what can a person achieve? Nothing, absolutely nothing! Without confidence, you can't even do an elementary thing like riding a bicycle.

Any religion that destroys self-confidence is sick. Healthy Christianity catches the central message that Jesus came and became the curse in our place, dying on the cross to restore our dignity, worth, and value. When our relationship with God is restored, we find our true selves. Jesus said so: "I am come that they might have life, and that they might have it more abundantly" (John 10:10 KJV).

Look at people who are lacking in confidence! They are tentative, unable to make important decisions. Drowning in a pool of self-doubt, they are defeated before the game starts. God did not create you to live life on the sidelines, but to win the game. If you long to stand out, to be a winner in the game of life, then this book is for you!

> Confidence is the necessary ingredient
> for a successful life.

On the other hand, we all know people who appear to be conceited. We say, "He has a big head," meaning he has an exaggerated opinion of himself. We get the impression that he doesn't need anyone. The Bible clearly warns about this attitude when it says, "Do not be conceited" (Romans 12:16). The Bible points out the sure consequences of thinking you can do it by yourself without God and other people when it says, "Pride goeth before destruction, and an haughty spirit before a fall" (Proverbs 16:18 KJV).

> God does not give His blessings to a person
> who thinks he can do it
> by himself.

You cannot afford to cling to conceit. It will ruin the good gifts that God gives you, destroy your relationships, and separate you from God. A healthy, happy, well-adjusted person lives with confidence without conceit. A person who possesses confidence without conceit is comfortable with himself and relates well to other people while he continues to grow and go for it. He is connected to a power greater than himself.

The Apostle Paul, out of his own testimony under the inspiration of the Holy Spirit, shared the secret of being a confident person without conceit when he said, "I can do all things through Christ which strengtheneth me" (Philippians 4:13 KJV). In the pages to come, we are going to explore how to put this key verse into practice in our daily lives. When we do this, we fulfill the purpose for which we were created and redeemed, and our lives bring glory to God.

> Give God the glory
> and He will be more than glad
> to share His glory with you.

It is my prayer that this book will capture the balance that's needed in the Christian community, in our thoughts and teachings on self-esteem. As Jesus said, "Without me ye can do nothing" (John 15:5 KJV). Within the context of this illustration of the vine and the branches, Jesus makes it clear that if we are connected to Him, wonderful things will happen and our lives will be fruitful.

I dedicate this book to my wife, Margaret Watson Galloway, affectionately known as Margi, who is a good example of a person connected to God who has this beautiful ingredient of confidence without conceit.

If you were to sit down and have a conversation with Margi, she would tell you that she has not always been a confident person. That would also be my personal testimony. If godly confidence can happen in our lives, then it can happen in your life. Because

> Nothing is impossible with God.

This book contains nineteen prime-time principles for successful living that, when understood and applied, will make you the cream that rises to the top. No matter what size container the cream exists in, sooner or later, it always rises to the top. With these nineteen prime-time principles taken from the Bible, you will find yourself rising to the top like cream, regardless of your circumstances or surroundings.

CONFIDENCE
Without Conceit

PART ONE

*Be a
Successful Person
in Your
World*

ONE

The Success Principle

Success is being the best person you can be—to the glory of God!

Sex! Money! Power! Most people are seeking these three things. One might ask, "If a person has sex, money, and power, is that person successful?" What do you think? The philosophy of the world, as portrayed on television, in magazines, and all around us seems to shout, "Yes!"

What is your philosophy of success? How would you personally define it? Someone has said: "If you have failed to consciously define a philosophy of success, you have unconsciously defined a philosophy of failure." You can ill afford to allow the world to dictate your philosophy of success. If you do, true success is going to pass you by like a ship that has set sail without you.

Where can a person go to learn the unchanging, unfailing principles of successful living? Every good success book that I have ever read took its principles from the one true and eternal book, the Bible. After years of studying the Scriptures and learning to apply the prime-time principles from the Bible, I have developed a personal philosophy of success that I believe is biblically based. This philosophy has been beautifully worked in needlepoint by one of my friends and hangs in the doorway of my office:

> **Success is being the best person
> you can be—to the glory of God!**

I strongly identify with basketball star Larry Bird, who says, "To me, a winner is someone who recognizes his God-given talents, works his tail off to develop them into skills, and uses those skills to accomplish his goals. Even when I lost, I learned what my weaknesses were, and I went out the next day to turn those weaknesses into strengths" (Larry Bird with John Bischoff, *Bird on Basketball*).

Five Enemies That Will Snatch
Success From You

Immorality   I would never hire a person whom I knew to be sexually immoral. Neither would I enter into a business agreement with an immoral person. The reason is simple: When people are immoral, they damage their character. You can't trust them, because they will lie. You are not going to get a full day's work out of them, because their energy and attention will be somewhere else. And they certainly are not going to have the power of God working through their lives.

> **God cannot bless immorality.**

What do I mean by immorality? I mean having sex with or desiring to have sex with any person to whom you are not married. Nothing destroys the bond and trust of marriage like immorality. Sex is a beautiful gift of God. We should cherish it and use it wisely. The right way to use it is in marriage. To use it carelessly outside of marriage is to abuse it.

In the Bible we read about King David, the most powerful man in his generation. He ruled over Israel, was admired, respected, and wealthy, and had beautiful wives. He had it all, and he lived in communion with God until he lusted after Bathsheba and committed adultery with her. Once caught in the web of immorality, not only did David lie, but he committed murder. Generations of deception, immorality, and murder came into his family and kingdom. David reaped the whirlwind of moral failure. His own sons rose up against each other and against him. The kingdom was torn apart because of David's immorality.

So serious and destructive is this sin that the Bible says to us:

Flee from sexual immorality. All other sins a man commits are outside his body, but he who sins sexually sins against his own body. Do you not know that your body is a temple of the Holy Spirit, who is in you, whom you have received from God? You are not your own; you were bought at a price. Therefore honor God with your body.

1 Corinthians 6:18–20

> Success is honoring God by living a clean life. Stand up and say no to the shame of immorality.

Imbalance   George Smith dedicated himself to being the president of a corporation. When his superiors said move, he moved. His work always came before his family. After years of neglect, his wife ran off with another man and his kids didn't want anything to do with him.

At last George crawled his way to the top and was made president of the company. Was he a success? Listen to what George said:

> The day I got all that I had dedicated myself to and worked so many long hours for was the most empty day of my life. I sat in my chair on the 42nd floor, alone, looking out the window. I realized that because I'd lived my life out of balance, although I had made it to the top in my company, I had no friends and no family. I asked myself, "What is all this worth if I don't have anyone to share it with?" I determined right there and then to spend the rest of my time on earth getting my life in balance, learning to love and relate to other people.

The Bible says it this way: "Let love be your greatest aim" (1 Corinthians 14:1 TLB).

Success is learning to live a balanced life.

Domination   Any person who misuses the power that God has entrusted to him by mistreating other persons will sooner or later experience a fall. One of the primary principles for living confidently without conceit is to treat other people as you want to be treated. This is not only the Golden Rule but the only way to get along with others. No one can have a successful life without getting along with others.

In every troubled home that I have ever known, a struggle is going on over power. Sometimes it is the husband, sometimes the wife, but often both are struggling over who is going to be in charge and then misusing that power. The Bible says that a man is successful when he treats his wife like his own body. A wife is successful when she treats her husband with honor and respect. Happy homes are where husbands and wives "Honor Christ by submitting to each other" (Ephesians 5:21 TLB). People who honor Christ by submitting to each other no longer feel they have to be in charge. When they are in charge, they want what is best for the other members of their family.

> **Successful people are those who give selfishness a kick in the pants.**

Greed I've known people without money who were just as greedy as people with money. Greed has nothing to do with the amount; it has to do with a person's attitude and spirit. You can't be greedy, grasping and clinging to possessions and money without becoming a slave to them. You were never created to be the slave of the things of this world.

God has chosen you and called you to be a steward, to receive from Him and give back to Him. Successful people are always generous givers, never selfish takers.

Forgetting God Without God, a person may be like a shooting star that makes a flash for a while but sooner or later self-destructs. There are people in our society who appear successful on the surface, but without God, they are really going nowhere fast. As the pilot of an airplane announced to his passengers, "Ladies and gentlemen, I have some good news and some bad news. The bad news is that our instrumentation has gone out and we don't know where we're going. The good news is that we have picked up a tail wind and are making good time!"

You can find true success if you will do as the Bible says: "In everything you do, put God first, and he will direct you and crown your efforts with success" (Proverbs 3:6 TLB).

Five Steps to Get You
on the Road to Success

Turn about-face   Someone said to me, "Pastor, it seems you like to spend your time with successful people."

I said to my friend, "I'd like to explain that to you. First, I like to spend my time with people who want to be everything they can be to the glory of God. Yes, I'll admit it: I spend time with people who see it big and go for it." But then I added, "Let me tell you something else. There is another kind of person I've spent a lot of time with. That's the person who does just what the Bible says and repents."

You see, it's not where you've been that's important; it's where you're going. I don't care what your failure or mistake has been. Jesus came so you could change, so you could get up and have a new start. But you need to understand that the word *repent* is a strong word. It means that you are sick and tired of sin and defeat and are going to change, with God's help. You are going to turn about-face. Instead of going the wrong way, you are going to get up and, with God's help, go the right way.

> With Christ's help, I am going to change.
> I am going to turn my past failures
> into stepping-stones to future success.

Commit to someone greater than you are   I am proud of the Gospel, of the Jesus life in me, for it is the power of God that makes a difference in my life. He gets me up when I am down. He keeps me going when I would give up. He makes me feel like a somebody when I feel like a nobody. The road to failure is paved with good intentions. The road to eternal success is gained by letting Jesus Christ become your Lord and live within you. ". . . Greater is he that is in you, than he that is in the world" (1 John 4:4 KJV).

Learn what is right and do it   People who fail in life are those who keep doing wrong. One of the things we're going to learn about is the principle of the harvest. When you make bad decisions, take bad actions, sow bad seeds, you reap bad results in your life. On the other hand, when you make right decisions, do what's right, and plant good seeds, you reap good results. You must take the responsibility for your own actions. Someone has rightly said, "A man is never a failure until he blames someone else."

Successful people go to the Word of God, learn what is right, and do it. In Proverbs 3:21 (TLB) we read these words: "Have two goals: wisdom—that is, knowing and doing right—and common sense. . . ." If you do this, you are going to have a very successful and prosperous life.

> **What I am to be,
> I now am becoming.**

See it big and go for it   One of the biggest sins that any person can commit is to waste his or her life by doing nothing.

Bob W. Ireland crossed the finish line on Thursday, November 6, 1986, as the New York City marathon's 19,413th and final finisher—the first person to run a marathon with his arms instead of his legs. Think of it! Bob is a forty-year-old

Californian whose legs were blown off in Vietnam seventeen years ago. He recorded the slowest time in the marathon's history: 4 days, 2 hours, 48 minutes, 17 seconds. When asked why he ran the race, he gave these three reasons: to show he was a born-again Christian, to test his conditioning, and to promote physical fitness for others. He said, "Success is not based on where you start, it's where you finish, and I finished."

What joy comes from seeing it big and going for it!

Do all you can, to the glory of God   I am convinced that we were created for the purpose of bringing glory to God. In fact, in the very first chapter of the Bible, we learn that we were created in the very image of God Himself.

For what purpose were we created?

- To live in poverty? No!
- To live in shame or low self-esteem? No!
- To waste our lives away? No!
- To be overcome, overrun, and defeated? No!

We were created to be successful, to fulfill our destinies, to bring glory to God through the tragedies and triumphs of our lives. When Jesus came to restore our lost glory, the Holy Spirit was given to us that we might glorify Jesus. Our purpose as Christians is to give glory to God, and I guarantee that if you determine to glorify God through your attitudes and actions, you will fulfill your destiny and be successful.

Life's greatest challenge is not being your own person but being God's person.

TWO

The Achiever's Principle

**Anything the mind can conceive
and I will dare to believe,
with God's help, I will achieve!**

God would never live a boring life! Somehow I cannot picture God resting in a rocking chair. I see Him as alert, creative, and involved in making things happen. God endowed you with creativity. You are made in such a way that you get great satisfaction from achieving. Don't ever apologize for wanting to achieve. Admit it, embrace it, go for it. Work hard for it, and enjoy whatever success comes to you!

Let me tell you one of my favorite stories from Dr. Norman Vincent Peale.

A college boy on the football team was a number-one goof-off. He liked to hear the cheers, but not to charge the line. He liked to wear the suit, but not to practice. One day the players were doing fifty laps, and this showpiece was doing his usual five. The coach came over and said, "Hey, kid, here is a telegram for you."

The kid said, "Read it for me, Coach." He was so lazy he did not even like to read.

The coach opened the telegram and read, "Dear Son, your father is dead. Come home immediately."

The coach swallowed hard. He said, "Take the rest of the week off." He didn't care if the kid took the rest of the year off; he was so unmotivated.

Game time came on Friday, and when the teams rushed out on the field, the last kid out was the goof-off. No sooner did the game begin than the kid said, "Coach, can I play today? Can I play?"

The coach thought, *Kid, you're not playing today. This is homecoming. This is the big game. We need every real guy we have, and you are not one of them.* But every time the coach turned around, the kid badgered him: "Coach, please let me play. Coach, I have got to play."

The first quarter ended with the score lopsided against the home team. At halftime, they were still further behind. The second half started, and things got progressively worse. The coach, mumbling to himself, began mentally writing out his resignation, when up came the kid. "Coach, Coach, let me play, please!"

The coach looked at the scoreboard. "All right," he said, "get in there, kid. You can't hurt anything now."

No sooner did the kid hit the field than his team exploded. He ran, blocked, and tackled like a star. The electricity leaped to the team. The score evened up. In the closing seconds of the game, this kid intercepted a pass and ran all the way for the winning touchdown!

The stands broke loose. The kid was everybody's hero. Such cheering you never heard. Finally the excitement subsided and the coach got over to the kid and said, "I never saw anything like that. What in the world happened to you out there?"

He said, "Coach, you know my dad died last week. My dad

was blind. But today, watching from heaven, he saw me play for the first time."

God is watching you from heaven to see what you will do with what He has given you. You say, "I don't have any talents!" That's not true. Maybe you have yet to discover your talent. Maybe you have put it on the shelf. But believe me, you have got some talents.

Why should you achieve? To bring out the best in you. To help other people. To enjoy a full and satisfying life. But most of all, to fulfill your destiny and be a good steward by making your life really count on this earth to the glory of God. I believe that every person has a mission in life. We must find that mission, work hard at it, and fulfill it. Our aim should be to do things that are worthwhile and influence other people's lives in a positive way, making their lives better. What are you doing to make the world a better place in which to live?

Conceive

All life, all achievement, begins with conception. Your life began at your conception. Jesus' life with us on this earth began with the virgin Mary's conception. We read in Matthew: " 'Joseph son of David, do not be afraid to take Mary home as your wife, because what is conceived in her is from the Holy Spirit. She will give birth to a son, and you are to give him the name Jesus, because he will save his people from their sins' " (Matthew 1:20, 21).

God has created our minds with ability to conceive and, according to Acts 2:17, the Holy Spirit transports the creative ideas of God to our minds. When we receive a great idea from God, a conception takes place. Visions and dreams are the language of the Holy Spirit. You can actually fellowship with the Holy Spirit, receive communication from God, and become pregnant with the seed of achievement.

To conceive and become pregnant with what it is that God wants you to achieve, two things must happen. First, you must visualize it. Second, holding that vision clear in your mind, you must begin to crystallize it. Recently I spoke to a group of ministers about our 20/20 Vision program, which involves training and equipping lay people to lead Tender Loving Care groups. The ministers asked me when I conceived this fantastic ministry that is achieving so much in helping people.

God began to plant the ideas in my mind way back in 1967, when I pastored a church in Lawrence, Kansas. It was a very old, traditional church. As a young pastor, I was very frustrated pastoring what I considered to be a dead church. So I began to pray, to read, and to ask God for answers. Into my mind came the seed thought of gathering together a few people for Bible study, prayer, and sharing. I began to invite some unchurched friends and a few nominal Christians to meet with me at a hotel for breakfast one morning a week. After we had met for about six or seven weeks, two of the men became Christians. It was exhilarating! It was exciting!

Crystallizing the idea more, I recruited a couple of young women in the church, shared my vision with them, and got them started leading small groups, reaching out to women in their neighborhoods.

When I started New Hope Community Church in 1972, I had the vision of many small groups. I crystallized that in a couple of ways. I set goals, because there are no worthwhile achievements without goals. How do you accomplish a big task? You divide it into small parts and get started. How do you build a cell ministry in a church? By starting one group at a time.

Over the years, this great vision conceived in my mind by the Holy Spirit has crystallized, until now we have "Super Bowl" training three times a year to bring in new recruits. We have weekly training and written lessons. We have district pastors who equip, encourage, and make our lay pastors successful. We are continually learning how to fulfill this great vision God has given to us. When your mind joins God's creative power through the Holy Spirit, wonderful things are achieved to the glory of God. "The intelligent man is always open to new ideas. In fact, he looks for them" (Proverbs 18:15 TLB).

Believe

> Believe: The magic word that transforms
> the impossible into the possible.

How important is it to believe? In John's Gospel alone, the word *believe* is used ninety-eight times. Belief is the key to making heaven your home. Belief is the key to knowing Jesus Christ personally. Belief is the key to tapping into the power of God. In John 20:31 we read, "But these are written that you may believe that Jesus is the Christ, the Son of God, and that by believing you may have life in his name."

I was recently reading Mark 9:23, 24, which is about the miraculous healing of a boy who was afflicted with an evil spirit. This boy's life was out of control. His behavior was so bizarre that he was destroying himself. The concerned, anxious father brought his son to Jesus. Jesus said to his father, "Everything is possible for him who believes." The Bible says, "Immediately the boy's father exclaimed, 'I do believe; help me overcome my unbelief!' " Then Jesus, through His power, which was the power of God, healed the boy.

Whenever our faith gets hooked up with Jesus, things that are greater than we are begin to happen in our lives. In the Christian faith, there is no room for the word *can't*. To stutter and stammer and excuse yourself by saying "I can't" is a denial of what Jesus wants to do through your life.

> **To be an achiever, you've got to
> not only eye it, but buy it!**

Before these wonderful things can happen through your life, you've got to buy in. Buy in to a personal relationship and fellowship with Jesus Christ. Fix your eyes on Jesus. What you can't do, Jesus can do through you, if you'll cooperate with Him.

Buy it! That simply means making the commitment. Make the commitment to Jesus Christ as Lord. Make the commitment that you are going to pay the price to achieve whatever God is calling you to achieve.

There is always a price to be paid for achievement. Following one of Paderewski's performances, a fan said to him, "I'd give my life to play like that."

The brilliant pianist replied, "I did!"

Buying it means discipline. It means saying yes when you need to say yes and saying no when you need to say no. It means you stop drifting and become selective. Any great achiever I've ever known has learned to deny the lesser to gain the greater.

To buy it is to really believe. To believe is to put faith ahead of your fears. Many a person has seen the vision, heard the call, then surrendered to fear and done nothing.

One of the saddest passages in the Bible is in Matthew 25. Here we read about a man who received an opportunity from his master but went and dug a hole and put his treasure in it. He decided to play it safe. He refused to take the risk. He caved in to his fears. When asked for an accounting by his master, the servant gave this pitiful excuse: ". . . I was afraid and went out and hid your talent in the ground . . ." (Matthew 25:25). His master was so furious that he cast the servant out for not doing something with his opportunity.

My friend, you need to know Jesus Christ so that belief comes alive within you. Then, with faith in Him, you will be able to stand up to your fears and move out to do what God is leading you to do.

> "I would rather attempt something
> great for God and fail,
> than do nothing and succeed."

I read recently a story about engineers in the lamp division of General Electric who were assigned what seemed to be the impossible task of frosting bulbs on the inside. At that time, no one believed this was really possible.

But an amazing thing happened. A newcomer by the name of Marion Pipkin, who didn't know the job was impossible, set to work and found a way to frost bulbs on the inside. Not only did he find a way to frost bulbs, but his process actually strengthened the bulbs. Remember, all things are possible if you believe.

Achieve

It's not enough just to see it by visualizing it. It's not enough just to believe it by verbalizing it. To achieve it, you have to go to work and do it.

As I was reading James 1:22, "But be ye doers of the word, and not hearers only . . ." (KJV), my eyes fell on the word *doers*. I remembered some simple and yet profound words my father often told me when I was a boy. "Son, do everything like it all depends upon you, and then trust God, like it all depends upon Him." I have tried to pattern my life after those wise words, and it has been most rewarding.

Nothing worthwhile is ever achieved until someone does something.

Do it again, only do it better   You failed one time, two times, three times. So what? What have you learned? How can you do it better? If God is calling you to do it and has given you the ability, then get up, begin again, and do it!

Use setbacks as stepping-stones to greater success.

Do what others are unwilling to do   The people who achieve are those who are willing to do whatever needs to be done. Since day one of our ministry at New Hope Community Church, there's no task that Margi and I have not done or are not willing to do. The success of our ministry comes from many people who would do anything and everything to achieve what God has called them to do.

Do it now   Procrastination is one of the worst enemies of achievement. Never put off until tomorrow what you can do today. Why delay? Time's wasting. Life is passing you by.

You have one life to live, so the time to spring into action is now. Do it *now!*

Never stop doing it   Because you are doing God's will does not mean it is going to be easy. Because you're doing what is right does not mean that storms will not come. If God has called you to do it, given it to you to do, then don't stop until you have somehow, someway, achieved it. Let your testimony be as Paul's: "I press toward the mark . . ." (Philippians 3:14 KJV).

I love these five immortal words that Winston Churchill carved into history. When it came to giving up, this is what Churchill had to say: "Never, never, never give up!"

> Anything the mind can conceive,
> and I will dare to believe,
> with God's help I will achieve.

THREE

The Confidence Principle

I am—I can!

Recently I read a story about a minister who had become depressed because of a very negative self-image. He was a senior pastor of a traditional, rigid church, and obviously things were not going well. Feeling defeated, he entered the sanctuary, knelt at the altar, and prayed, "Oh, God, I am nothing. I am a worm. I can't do anything right." Over and over he repeated these degrading words.

His associate walked by and was very impressed by what the senior pastor was praying. He joined him and also prayed, "Oh, Lord, I'm nothing. I am a worm. I can't do anything right."

While the two ministers were praying, the custodian happened to walk by and overhear them. Impressed, he went in, knelt beside them, and repeated the same prayer: "Oh, Lord, I, too, am nothing. I am a worm. I can't do anything right."

The associate pastor stopped praying, looked over at the

custodian, then turned to the senior pastor and whispered, "What's he doing, praying like us? Who does he think he is, anyway?"

We laugh at this little story because it's so true to life. But the sad thing is that whenever and however a human being is degraded, personal relationships go downhill. Dr. Joyce Brothers, well-known author, columnist, and psychologist, says, "An individual's self-concept is the core of his personality. It affects every aspect of human behavior: the ability to learn, the capacity to grow and change, the choice of friends, mates, and careers. It is no exaggeration to say that a strong, positive self-image is the best possible preparation for success in life."

Great numbers of people are suffering from a lack of confidence resulting from low self-esteem. They feel inferior. They are full of fear and do not believe in themselves.

The Bible teaches us not only to believe in God but to believe in ourselves because God is with us. The Bible stresses the importance of confidence when it says, "So do not throw away your confidence; it will be richly rewarded" (Hebrews 10:35). In Isaiah 30:15 (KJV) we read, ". . . In quietness and confidence shall be your strength. . . ."

The other day someone asked me, "Pastor, is it possible to have too much confidence?" Yes, it is. We all run across people with big egos who praise and parade themselves in front of others. Their arrogance, cockiness, and downright conceit turn us off. There is something obnoxious about people who have to go around telling everyone how wonderful, marvelous, and terrific they are.

Is it possible to have confidence without conceit? Yes, it is. The most beautiful people I've ever known have had confidence without conceit. Jesus Christ is a perfect example of One who had confidence without conceit. Jesus knew who He was. He said, "I am the resurrection, and the life . . ." (John 11:25 KJV). Yet, this same Jesus, a man of sureness and confidence, was also the model for servanthood. Not only did He say, "But he that is greatest among you shall be your servant" (Matthew 23:11 KJV), but this was the way He lived His life.

When I think of confidence without conceit, I think of Jesus, and the people I have known on this earth who have been most like Jesus have been people who had confidence without conceit. To have confidence without conceit, you have to know God personally. You also have to know who you are as a child of God and fulfill your role as a servant.

How to Have Confidence Without Conceit

I am a divine creation   Say it. You begin to build your self-confidence when you believe that you are made by a loving Master Creator.

Standing on the windswept shores of Lake Michigan one windy night, ready to throw himself into the freezing water, a thirty-two-year-old banker happened to gaze up at the starry heavens. Suddenly he felt a rush of awe, and this thought flashed through his mind: *You have no right to eliminate yourself. You do not belong to you. You belong to the universe.*

R. Buckminster Fuller turned his back on the lake and began a remarkable career. Best known as the inventor of the geodesic dome, by the time of his death, he held more than 170 patents and was world famous as an engineer, mathematician, architect, and poet.

Buckminister Fuller's experience that night on Lake Michigan echoes and affirms the ancient psalmist who, when contemplating the glory of God's creation, wrote these words: "When I consider your heavens, the work of your fingers, the moon and the stars, which you have set in place, what is man that you are mindful of him, the son of man that you care for him?" (Psalms 8:3, 4.)

The psalmist was inclined to feel insecure and inadequate in the face of such magnificence, but he wrote a resounding reply to his own question: "You made him a little lower than the heavenly beings and crowned him with glory and honor" (Psalms 8:5).

Like it or not, you are God's greatest creation, and with that comes responsibility as well as glory.

I am different from you   In Galatians 6:4 we read these words: ". . . Then he can take pride in himself, without comparing himself to somebody else." Be proud of who you are. You are unique and different. You look different, your personality is different, your temperament is different. There's no one else on this whole earth just like you. Don't commit the sin of comparing yourself with others. Accept yourself and start succeeding at being you.

For example, if you think you're fat, instead of comparing yourself and putting yourself down, decide what you want to weigh. There are only two acceptable choices. If you think you need to lose weight, then lose weight. On the other hand, if you don't want to lose weight, accept yourself as you are and like yourself as you are.

I am a forgiven child of God   Nothing destroys confidence as much as unforgiven sin. The Bible tells us, "For all have sinned, and come short of the glory of God" (Romans 3:23 KJV). Everyone has skeletons in the closet.

Thank God for Jesus, who came and died on the cross for our complete forgiveness. The difference between the saint and the sinner is not that one has sinned and the other hasn't. The difference is that God's grace and forgiveness have dealt with the sin in the life of the saint.

Thank God that when we ask for forgiveness, ". . . he is faithful and just to forgive us our sins, and to cleanse us from all unrighteousness" (1 John 1:9 KJV).

The Apostle Paul is a classic example of a man who had confidence without conceit. His life certainly was not without sin. Prior to his conversion, he had persecuted and killed Christians. Yet this forgiven child of God declared, "There is therefore now no condemnation to them which are in Christ Jesus . . ." (Romans 8:1 KJV).

I am not perfect—but I am forgiven. Make this your testimony, and be thankful for what He has done for you in Jesus.

I am a member of God's family   One of the things that really builds confidence and strength is knowing that we are part of a big family. As Christians, we belong to one another. Wherever you may go, the world over, there is a network of Christians to which you belong. The ancient rabbis were right when they said, "Anyone who goes too far alone goes mad." I am so glad that I'm part of the family of God.

We really do need one another!

Cultivate people who help you grow. Make friends with people who will bring out the best in you and make you feel comfortable with who you are. Find people who will rejoice with you when you rejoice and weep with you when you weep. To have this kind of friend, you need to be this kind of friend.

I am a human being with strengths and weaknesses The Apostle Paul really hits it on the head when he says, ". . . Do not think of yourself more highly than you ought, but rather think of yourself with sober judgment, in accordance with the measure of faith God has given you" (Romans 12:3).

To paraphrase this, don't puff yourself up. Don't run yourself down, either. Instead, have a sensible, sane view of yourself. Like everyone else, you have certain strengths and certain weaknesses. The good news is, Jesus accepts you just as you are. Now accept yourself and, with Christ's help, build on your strengths and eliminate your weaknesses.

Affirmations That
Help You Have Confidence Without Conceit

I can change the way I think about myself Consider this man, who had several strikes against him. As a boy, he was extremely thin and painfully shy. Practically every other member of his family was an accomplished public speaker.

"I was shy and bashful," he says, "and this self-image of inadequacy might have gone on indefinitely had it not been for something a professor said to me during my sophomore year in college. One day, after I had made a miserable showing, he told me to wait after class. 'How long are you going to be bashful like this, scared rabbit, afraid of the sound of your own voice?' he demanded. 'You'd better change the way you think about yourself, Peale, before it's too late.' "

That may sound like a strong dose of medicine for a young man, but it worked. The boy's name was Norman Vincent Peale, and he went on to become one of America's greatest preachers and writers. Some of you are asking if you can change. Yes, with Christ's help, you can stand up to your fears with courage and confidence. But first, you've got to change your self-talk. Stop telling yourself what you can't do, and start telling yourself what you can do, with Christ's help.

I can be confident without conceit   How can you be a person who has confidence without conceit? The answer to this momentous question is found in Jesus' reply to the Pharisee's question concerning which of the commandments was the greatest. Jesus answered: " 'Love the Lord your God with all your heart and with all your soul and with all your mind.' This is the first and greatest commandment. And the second is like it: 'Love your neighbor as yourself' " (Matthew 22:37–39).

Here are the two secrets of self-confidence without conceit: worship and serving others.

Worship causes us to look upward to God and not at ourselves. When we praise God for who He is and what He does, we are expressing our love and commitment to God. When we are worshiping God, we are not engaging in the kind of self-worship that leads to self-deception and conceit.

All the wonderful people I have known who had confidence without conceit were happily serving others. They were putting into practice Jesus' commandment to love their neighbors as themselves.

The amazing thing about confidence is that it comes from losing yourself in something greater than yourself. Whenever we start to grab for self-confidence for its own sake, it's like trying to grab smoke. The confidence that Jesus wants us to have is the by-product of worship and service. As we lose ourselves in Christ and live lives of service, we come to realize that we are comfortable and confident with who we are and what we are doing.

> Love given and love received
> always yield confidence without conceit.

I can do something well   While it is true that our primary worth should come from who we are, it is also true that we were made to do something, to accomplish something. As someone has said, "Somewhere under the stars God has a job for you to do, and nobody else can do it." You may have to go down a lot of dead-end streets before you find what it is you are good at, but it's there.

At New Hope Community Church we keep asking people, "What are your gifts?" Or we ask, "What is God calling you to do?" We challenge people to find how God wants to use their lives to bless others. There is something you can do or can learn to do that will bless others and really make you feel good about yourself.

> Help your kids find something
> they can excel in.

In *Hide or Seek* Dr. James Dobson told about his junior-high-school years, when he was skinny, shy, and not very popular. One day his father took him out on the tennis court to teach him how to play tennis. Dobson describes how he got bored with it and did not want to practice. But his dad kept his thumb in his son's back. They went out there on Saturday mornings to practice. Later he became glad his father had, because when he was in high school, that ability boosted his self-confidence. If asked to write an essay on the subject, "Who Am I?" one positive thing he could have said was, "I am the best tennis player in my school."

I can help other people be successful   An old drunk was brought into the hospital on the West Side of New York. A doctor who had seen him there many times before took him aside, looked at him in disgust, and said, "Do you know this is the fifteenth time you've been in this hospital for the treatment of alcoholism?"

The old drunk responded, "Well, I think that calls for a celebration. How about a drink?"

As the doctor just shook his head, the obnoxious drunk continued, "What's the matter, doc? Am I hopeless? Give me a drink."

"All right," the doctor said, "I'll tell you what I'll do. I'll give you a drink on one condition."

"Tell me what it is. I'll do it! Anything for a drink," the drunk answered.

The doctor said, "There's a young man down at the end of the hall. He's about nineteen. This is the first time he's been in here for treatment. I want you to go down and pay him a visit. I want him to take a good look at you. Maybe he won't take the road you've taken."

The old drunk was shocked at this and said, "You mean you'll give me a drink if I do that?"

The doctor said yes, so the old drunk staggered down the hall into the young man's room. He looked at the clean-cut young man and began to talk to him. "You know, boy," he said, "you don't want to turn out the way I did. I was young like you once. I had a mother who loved me and a father who had dreams for me. To look at me now, you wouldn't believe it, but once I even had dreams for myself."

Something happened inside the old drunk. The more he talked to this young man, the more he felt he had a mission in life. He had to save this youth from the tortured, miserable life he had experienced. They talked all morning. Finally, they made a pact. The old man said, "I'll tell you what I'll do, boy. If you ever need a drink, you call me. Okay? I'll help you get through without it." The boy agreed to do the same for the old man.

That was the turning point in the life of Bill, who founded Alcoholics Anonymous. When he shared his life to save another, he was saved.

I can do things to the glory of God Have you ever felt inferior? I guess each of us has felt inferior sometime. But let me tell you something: God didn't create you inferior to anyone. He created you in His own image, as a worthwhile person with the ability to do things to the glory of God.

Have you ever seen a picture of a newborn thoroughbred colt? He stands in an awkward, gangly fashion, but it is obvious that he is a thoroughbred, a race horse. Within him is the ability to run with the wind. We are all like that colt. We are bred to run, created to achieve, destined for success. It is in our very bloodline, part of our makeup. It is the birthright and heritage that God gave us when He designed us.

Six Ways to Do Things for the Glory of God

Do what you can do You are not like anyone else. Your opportunities are different. Right in front of you are things that you can begin to do right now. If you do what you have been given to do, you will begin to be successful.

Bloom where you are planted.

Do it more often People who achieve great things are not usually any smarter or more gifted than anyone else. Great people are ordinary people with an extra amount of determination. They do what they can do, they do what others are unwilling to do, and they do it more often. They are diligent, faithful, steady, and stable. When someone else is playing, they are working. In athletics, when team practice is over, they practice more. In marriage, they give 100 percent. In church, they are not spectators; they are participators. At work, they don't watch the clock, they get the job done.

Do something greater than you have ever done before The way to overcome a failure is to use it as a stepping-stone to success. So what if you have failed here or there? Learn all you can from your experiences, get up, and do it better than ever. Dream a new dream. Do something greater than you have ever done before. You were not made to wallow around in failure; you were made to get up and do something greater, to the glory of God.

Do it now! Procrastination is your worst enemy. Before you can cross the finish line, you've got to leave the starting line. You've been thinking about it. You've been dreaming about it. The time to get up and get started is now!

Do what it takes, depending on Christ's strength to achieve My favorite verse, the one I want to live by, is Philippians 4:13 (KJV): "I can do all things through Christ which strengtheneth me." That's the key to living life. Pull out all the stops and, with Christ's help, go for it! With Christ's power and strength, you can achieve things you never dreamed possible.

When I was growing up, my dad was church administrator for 140 churches. During those years I witnessed a repeated phenomenon in some of these churches. A given church would struggle along, showing no signs of growth and not much life.

The pastor and leadership didn't expect much to happen, and consequently nothing did.

Then a young pastor or a seasoned veteran of faith and vision would be called to that struggling church. He would come in believing that nothing was impossible. He would believe that God could help him and the people do wonderful things. He would plunge in and get started on fulfilling the vision and the dream. Before long, that church would come alive, begin to grow, and draw unchurched people to Christ through its fellowship. Nothing is impossible with Christ's strength.

Do it all for the glory of God   In 1 Corinthians 10:31 we read, "So whether you eat or drink or whatever you do, do it all for the glory of God." This is an exciting way to live. This is the way to fulfill your destiny. This is the way to feel really good about yourself. This is the way to do God's will through your life on this earth.

If we do something to glorify God, we glorify Him most when we do it best. In this world we are God's representatives; other people judge God by what they see in us.

Jesus said it this way, ". . . let your light shine before men, that they may see your good deeds and praise your Father in heaven" (Matthew 5:16).

FOUR

The Championship Principle

The difference between a chump and a champ is dedication!

A person cannot achieve success in a vocation, a marriage, or athletics without dedication. A person cannot achieve financially or in ministry without dedication. Most of all, you cannot live the Christian life without a lot of dedication. This is why Jesus said, "If anyone would come after me, he must deny himself and take up his cross and follow me. For whoever wants to save his life will lose it, but whoever loses his life for me and for the gospel will save it" (Mark 8:34, 35).

Every winner that I've known has been a dedicated person. Do you know who is our greatest example of dedication? He is the winner of all winners—Jesus! Hebrews 12 teaches us how to win the race. We are to fix our eyes on Jesus, our example and leader, and follow in His steps. "Consider him who endured such opposition from sinful men, so that you will not grow weary and lose heart" (v. 3). Look at Him ". . . who for the joy set before him endured the cross, scorning its shame : . . ." (v. 2). Because Jesus was so dedicated to carrying out the will of God to save us, He was victorious.

> There is nothing you cannot do
> if you are totally dedicated to Christ
> and to doing what's worthwhile on this earth.

Choose What Is Worthwhile

If we could sit down and talk, and you could tell me what you're dedicated to and what you're not dedicated to, I could predict what your life holds for you. For the best in life, you must dedicate yourself to that which has the most value. What has true and lasting value in this world?

Watch out, because Satan is the author of confusion. The fact that we live in a world of very confused and mixed-up values is evidence of his work. So many people are throwing their lives away on things that are worthless and, in many cases, destructive.

The first step in getting your priorities straight is to get right with God. In the Scriptures we read these words: "In everything you do, put God first, and he will direct you and crown your efforts with success" (Proverbs 3:6 TLB). True success begins with commitment to God and living out a life of putting Him first in everything. This in itself takes the confusion away. On this solid rock you can begin to build the other things to which you want to dedicate your life. For example, I'm dedicated to my wife and our marriage. I'm dedicated to my children and our family. I'm dedicated to the success of my church. I'm dedicated to helping other people.

Commit yourself to these wonderful things in life and you

will have a wonderful life. Do you have your priorities straight today? If not, come into the Lord's presence and get them straightened out. There is nothing worse than living your life with mixed-up priorities. What a waste!

> Dedication to Christ first gives one
> the perspective and strength to achieve
> what one cannot achieve any other way.

Fix Your Sights on the Target

Jesus was successful. He endured, overcame, and triumphed because He had His heart and mind fixed on the target. "He steadfastly set his face to go to Jerusalem" (Luke 9:51 KJV). Jerusalem was where He would be put to death on the cross.

What you need is a similar fixation on your target. Our primary target should be to make heaven our home and take everybody we can with us, and while we are here on earth, to achieve the good things that God calls us to achieve for His glory.

Let me illustrate the importance of setting goals. Steve's burning ambition was to coach his high school basketball team to a state championship. His dream became the dream of each of his players. The boys gave up their summer to play basketball for hours every day. As fall came, they gave up going out for football so they would be ready when the basketball season opened. These boys even gave up going out with girls so they would not be distracted from winning the state championship.

Basketball season opened with the team winning, and each game was one more victory in their march toward the crown. Then came the big deciding game; if they won that one, they would be state champions. They charged out of the locker room, almost tearing the door off its hinges as they ran onto the court.

Abruptly, they stopped in their tracks in complete confusion, frustration, and anger. The hoops had been removed! Everyone knows that you can't play a basketball game without goals to aim for.

How about you? Are you trying to play the game of your life without goals? If you are, it is no wonder that you are frustrated!

Pay the Price

The achievement of anything worthwhile has its price. Few things grow overnight without any effort. Toadstools do, but they're not worth much. In the Christian faith, which is the greatest thing in this world, there is a price to be paid.

There is no feast without a sacrifice.

How much do you really want to win the race? How badly do you want to reach your worthwhile goal? If you have a take-it-or-leave-it attitude, the odds are that when the bill comes, you'll leave it.

How dedicated are you to Christ?

- Enough to serve Him?
- Enough to pay your tithe?
- Enough to live a clean life?
- Enough to love that person anyway?
- Enough to put away that dirty habit?
- Enough to go for the gold to His glory?

A while back I was counseling a talented, handsome young man whom I admire. He was having a lot of difficulty in his marriage with the typical problems that a lot of young marriages go through but which were very serious for him and his wife. They were separated, and it was painful.

But they were teachable. I said to the young man, "If you want to have a good marriage—and that is a worthwhile goal—then this is what you have to do. Do whatever you have to do to win your wife back. Make any adjustment. Change whatever you have to change. Do whatever you have to do." He went out and did just that, and now, instead of having a failing marriage, he has a successful, happy marriage. Yes, the difference between a chump and a champ is dedication.

> Strip off anything and everything
> that holds you back.

The Bible tells us, ". . . let us throw off everything that hinders and the sin that so easily entangles, and let us run with perseverance the race marked out for us" (Hebrews 12:1). Eliminate the negative. Whatever is holding you back, pulling you down, defeating you—throw it off! This includes past mistakes and the fear of failure.

Concentrate on Jesus! The Bible says, "Let us fix our eyes on Jesus, the author and perfecter of our faith . . ." (Hebrews 12:2). Get your eyes off defeat and on the Victor. We are more than conquerors through Him that loved us.

Use Positive Self-Discipline in a New, Positive Way

Self-discipline is something that everybody needs but not too many people want. Unfortunately, the very word *discipline* puts us off because it sounds restrictive or like punishment. It is important that we understand discipline. Discipline is not something we do because we want to feel bad. Discipline is not an end in itself. Discipline is something we do in order to achieve a greater purpose.

> **Without self-discipline, there can be no worthwhile achievement.**

The Bible says it this way: "To win the contest you must deny yourselves many things that would keep you from doing your best . . ." (1 Corinthians 9:25 TLB). Discipline is denying the lesser things to gain the greater ones.

The whole world of achievement belongs to the person who will put forth the willpower to discipline himself. It is self-discipline that makes the mind sharp and quick. It is the self-disciplined body that has more energy and zest and keeps going when others wear out. A self-disciplined person has learned to control his emotions and keep his cool when all others lose their heads. Self-discipline can shape you up until you feel like a champ instead of a chump.

One place we need self-discipline is in prayer. Everyone has a desire to pray. To talk to God and have Him talk to you is sweet communion. Then why don't we do it more? Because it's not going to happen without discipline.

Get the Help You Need From Jesus

Dear Pastor Galloway,

Friday we will be celebrating our fifth wedding anniversary. To some people this would not be such an eventful occasion, but to us this is an accomplishment achieved only by the help of the Lord. The reason we are writing to you is to thank you for believing in us and giving us the tools to rebuild our lives.

If you recall, we came to you over five years ago for marriage counseling, as we wanted you to marry us. Dick and I had been divorced, and we both had many scars and deep hurts. We were very much in love, but we were going to enter a second marriage with many, many problems.

Pastor Galloway, you were honest with us and told us we had a very hard road ahead, going into a marriage with so many problems. You told us that in order to withstand all of the problems we were facing, we would have to put God as the head of our household.

On September 25, 1982, you married us in your office, with only our six children and a witness for each of us present. This was the happiest day of our lives, but reality set in quite rapidly, and the problems began. The dreams we shared were becoming nightmares, and the harder we tried (and I stress the word *we*), the more the marriage seemed to be doomed.

Dick and I were very unhappy. We knew we loved each other very much, but we just could not go on living like this. I remember one Sunday morning you greeted us with a smile and asked how we were doing. I immediately started to cry and told you things were not good and to pray for us.

I can't say exactly when things started to get better, but I can tell you why things started to change. One night Dick and I asked the Lord to intervene, take our marriage, and use it for the glory of God. We both are very stubborn, but we had had enough, and we totally submitted our lives to the Lord. Ever since we both submitted, the blessings have not stopped pouring in. Our marriage is on very solid ground, we have a wonderful blended family that we are very proud of, our finances are beyond belief, and the Lord found a job for me that is much better than the one I had before. Dick has been attending Western Baptist Seminary for the last three years and will graduate this year with his masters in Christian counseling. Even though our schedule is crazier than when we first got married, everything falls into place because we are faithful to God's direction.

We know that Jesus has pulled us out of the clutches of Satan himself, and we will proclaim the victory forever and ever. If you submit to the Lord and are faithful to Him, all things are possible.

FIVE
The Leadership Principle

Set the sail.

A couple of months ago I said to one of my fellow pastors on the staff, "As you work with people, you'll find that they have their ups and downs. The tide goes out and the tide comes in. On any given day, you can find people who are discouraged and defeated. If you allow them to set the tone, you are going to be defeated. To be the leader and achieve what you should to the glory of God, you must set the sail."

Moses was a gifted leader, but in Numbers we find that he failed miserably because he did not set the sail. God had raised him up to lead the children of Israel out of Egypt, across the wilderness, and into the Promised Land. Did you ever wonder why they wandered for forty years in the wilderness when it was a fairly short journey across the desert to the Promised Land? It was not God's plan for them to wander in the wilderness for forty years; they wandered because they did not set the sail and stick with God's plan.

After a short period of time, they were at the edge of the Promised Land. Moses, without making a decision to take the land, made the mistake of sending out an exploration party of twelve men. Like so many committees, instead of looking for ways to take the Promised Land, they looked at all the reasons it was impossible. When they came back, ten of them gave negative reports. Only Joshua and Caleb wanted to march in and take the land. The ten negative committee members made everyone else negative, and Moses was powerless to move the people.

In Numbers 14 we read how God was pleased with Caleb and Joshua for their faith and honored that by promising that they and their children would see the Promised Land.

But then, beginning in verse 32, we read what God told Moses and the negative people:

" 'But you—your bodies will fall in this desert. Your children will be shepherds here for forty years, suffering for your unfaithfulness, until the last of your bodies lies in the desert. For forty years—one year for each of the forty days you explored the land—you will suffer for your sins and know what it is like to have me against you.' I, the Lord, have spoken, and I will surely do these things to this whole wicked community, which has banded together against me. They will meet their end in this desert; here they will die."

Numbers 14:32–35

After being such a great leader for so many years, Moses failed miserably because he did not act decisively and set the sail. He surrendered his leadership to grumbling, complaining, negative people. When he did so, he stepped out of the will of God.

After Moses died, God raised up Joshua to lead the people, and he set the sail. He made a decision because it was the right thing to do—it was what God had called him to do. Then, after making the decision, he set out to solve the problems.

> **First you make the decision,
> then you solve the problems.**

In Joshua 1:10, 11 we read these words: "So Joshua ordered the officers of the people: 'Go through the camp and tell the people, "Get your supplies ready. Three days from now you will cross the Jordan here to go in and take possession of the land the Lord your God is giving you for your own." ' "

Then, after having made the decision and telling the people to get ready, Joshua chose two spies he could trust and sent them ahead to explore and see how—not *whether*—they could take the land. They then proceeded to conquer the land through the power of God.

> **Success is a process.**

If you have had disappointments and failures in your life, then learn from your failures and move ahead to do something greater for God. He didn't create you to be a loser. He created you to be a winner.

I like the slogan that George Halas, former coach of the Chicago Bears, had displayed on his office wall: ALWAYS GO TO BED A WINNER. Let's not take any attitude of defeat into tomorrow with us. Let's get rid of it. Let God take it, and go into the future believing the best is yet to come.

The only way to have the best in the future is to set the sail. Otherwise, you'll never get where you want to go. I think of

Christopher Columbus when he wanted to sail west to Asia, believing the world was round. "Oh, no," everyone else said, "the world is flat." But Christopher Columbus set the sail.

To be successful in the future, to get the most out of your life, *set the sail.* How do you do that? Here are five steps necessary to set the sail.

Sight the Port

Before you can go anywhere, you have to have a vision of where you want to go. Without a clear-cut vision, you will just drift.

Helen Keller was once asked what could be worse than being born blind. She replied, "To have sight and no vision." The Bible says, "Where there is no vision, the people perish . . ." (Proverbs 29:18 KJV). Life is a boring waste without a vision. But with a vision, life becomes exciting; every day is a new adventure.

The happiest people in the world are those who are living out their dreams. They have given themselves to something bigger than they are. They are going for something better than what they have now. They are depending on God to accomplish what they cannot do themselves. For an exciting life, hitch your wagon to a beautiful dream: Sight the port—and go for it!

At New Hope Community Church, we are in the process of realizing a great dream that God has given to us, a dream to reach this unchurched city for Jesus Christ. Together we have been experiencing the joy of realizing our God-given dream. Our first dream was to have a thousand members by our tenth anniversary. We realized that dream five years ago. Our second dream was to have four thousand members at fifteen years. A few weeks ago, we achieved that dream.

Now our dream is to double our membership and every one

of our need-meeting ministries in the next three years. We will go from four thousand members to eight thousand members. Some eighty percent of the people that join New Hope Community Church have been unchurched. We are reaching out in love to reach the unchurched—healing hurts and building dreams.

Our vision is crystallized in what we call the 20/20 Vision. In Acts 20:20 we read these words: "You know that I have not hesitated to preach anything that would be helpful to you but have taught you publicly and from house to house." At New Hope Community Church, we have these great celebrations every Sunday. Then during the week we get together from house to house and place to place with lay people as leaders in life-changing ministry. We call these leaders lay pastors. We call these groups Tender Loving Care groups.

Right now we have 400 lay pastors and 300 TLC groups. Weekly, 3,400 people attend these groups. The God-given vision communicated into my heart in recent months, through the Holy Spirit, is that we will double our number of lay pastors, TLC groups, and the number of people in these thriving, alive groups in the next three years.

This past year God has placed in my heart a vision that we would share our ministry with other churches. Our goal is to make other churches successful in reaching the unchurched. Recently Floyd Schwanz, who gives outstanding leadership to our Church Growth Institute in helping other churches be successful, reported that 106 churches that we know of have caught our 20/20 Vision and are using our model in their ministry. These 106 churches now have 996 Tender Loving Care groups that they call by a variety of names. There are probably 10,000 people in these cell groups. My vision is that this will double every year in the next three years in other churches. When that happens, with our own growth, plus the multiplication in other churches, we will see, three years from now, 100,000 people in Tender Loving Care groups.

> **There is a difference between just being a dreamer and having a God-given dream.**

Only one thing is worse than living life without a vision: to have had a dream and lost it. When David had a vision, he conquered Goliath. When he lost his vision, he couldn't conquer his own lust. When Alexander the Great had a vision, he conquered countries. When he lost it, he couldn't conquer the liquor bottle. When Solomon had a vision, he was the wisest man in the world. When he lost the dream God had given him, he couldn't control his own life.

The time has come for you to dream a new dream. Vision always comes before victory. The Bible says, ". . . You do not have, because you do not ask God" (James 4:2). Ask for and receive God's dream for your life.

Chart the Course

Today is the day to dream God's dream. Today is the day to stop and plan for the future. It is better to look ahead and prepare than look back and regret. You not only need to think out your goals, but you need to give them detail. Goals are a way of crystallizing the vision.

A passenger was talking to the captain of the *Queen Mary* during an ocean cruise. He asked the captain, "How long would it take you to stop this vessel?"

The captain replied, "If I shut down all the engines, it would take me a little over a mile to get this vessel completely stopped." He added, "A good captain thinks at least a mile ahead."

The older I become, the more I see how important it is to take the time to plan. The more time spent in planning, the higher the percentage of success. What are your goals for your family? What are your goals in business? What are your goals in school? What are your goals in your Christian life? What are your goals in your prayer life? What are your goals in your ministry? What is it that you plan to achieve that you can't do without the power of God working through your life?

Follow the Captain's Orders

The young man had just been made captain and assigned his first ship in the navy. He had an inflated ego that hadn't yet adjusted to his new position. They were sailing at night on their charted course when a message came over the radio: "Turn right ten degrees. You are headed for collision."

The message was given to the young captain. In his arrogance he decided he wouldn't change course for anyone. After all, he was in charge. The captain ordered this message sent: "You turn right ten degrees. I am the captain!"

Back came the communication: "*You* turn right ten degrees. *I am the lighthouse!*"

> For your ship to get to the right destination,
> you can only have one Master,
> and that is Jesus Christ.
> Jesus is Lord.

Recently I was reading Romans 6 through 8 and chapter 12. There is a word that Paul uses again and again to describe the right relationship with God: *yield*. This word is translated from a military word that meant "to be in the king's army, yielded to his command and direction." To yield means to obey our Commander-in-Chief without reservation.

Are you yielded completely to God? Yielding is something you do once and for all. It is also something you have to keep doing in your daily life. Those who are yielded to Jesus follow His commands explicitly. They have a burning desire to make their lives count for Jesus. They yearn to glorify Jesus. What is the desire of your heart?

A yielded life plugs into a power that is greater than we are. Jesus said that we would do greater things than these (*see* John 14:12). How is this possible? Through a life yielded completely to the control and power of the Holy Spirit.

Move Ahead With Singleness of Purpose

How badly do you want to realize your God-given dream? What price are you willing to pay? What are you willing to give up for it? To fulfill the dream, you must have singleness of purpose. You must concentrate and focus on the dream as the priority of your life. You can expect problems. Nothing worthwhile is without problems. The greater the dream, the greater the obstacles. God created you to be a problem solver; when faced with a problem, look for a solution.

The one gift that my eleven-year-old son, Scott, wanted more than anything else was a remote-controlled car. A couple of days before Christmas, we let him open the gift. Boy, was he excited! His joy overflowed. Scott couldn't wait to get the car out and running. A part of getting this car going was to put a small string through a fifteen-inch tube that would be the aerial on the car. Scott and I must have worked for an hour trying to get the string through the tube. It was a tight fit.

I've often repeated the old saying, "Inch by inch, anything's a cinch." Well, here it was fingernail by fingernail. Somehow we were going to push that string through. We twisted, pushed, turned, shoved, moaned. There was no way either he or I was going to give up.

After about forty minutes, we had the string about halfway through the tube, but it would go no further. I started thinking creatively. In every problem, look for the solution. There's got to be a way—somehow, somewhere!

"Scott, go get me a bar of soap with a little water on it." Scott came back with the soap, resisting the idea, sure that soap couldn't do anything to help us. I started soaping the string, and it went in a little bit better, but I still wasn't getting very far. Then I pulled the whole string out of the tube, soaped the whole string, and within a minute or two, I had it through the tube. We had the aerial up, and the turbo car was ready to race on command.

The Scriptures tell us that when we need wisdom, we should ask for it. The promise is that God will give us wisdom and insight. He will help us solve our problems.

Sail on With Persistence

So many people never realize their dream because when the going gets tough, they give up. When the going gets tough, the tough get going. When tough times come, rely on the strength and power of Jesus. When I am tempted to give up, I often think of those words that were spoken of Columbus when he was facing fierce storms and mutiny: "Brave admiral, what do we say when all hope is gone?" Back come the words like a leaping sword, "Sail on, sail on, and on."

Remember Jesus, who steadfastly set his face to go to Jerusalem. Thank God He didn't give up, even though it cost Him His own blood to fulfill God's dream for our lives. Let us be like our Lord, steadfast, unmovable, always abounding in the work of the Father.

PART TWO

*Be Successful
in All Your
Relationships*

SIX

The VIP Principle

"Treat others as you want them to treat you"
(Luke 6:31 TLB).

Your success and happiness depend on your learning and putting into practice the VIP (very important person) principle. This principle is guaranteed to help you in all your relationships with others.

Right across the freeway from our church is the area's largest shopping center, which contains one of the most successful retail chains in the nation, one known as a pacesetter in customer service. I recently saw a poster in that store that read, THE ONLY DIFFERENCE BETWEEN STORES IS THE WAY THEY TREAT THEIR CUSTOMERS. This store's stock has multiplied many times in the last several years; its sales keep going up and up. Why? Because they keep teaching their employees to give their customers the VIP treatment.

Jesus gave us the perfect principle for getting along well with other people: the Golden Rule. Near the end of the Sermon on the Mount, Christ summed up all the profound teachings on human relationships by saying, "Treat others as you want them to treat you" (Luke 6:31 TLB). In this VIP principle, Christ teaches us two things about successful relationships with others:

- The way to understand someone and get along well with him is to put yourself in his place.
- The way to win friends and influence people is to treat every person as you want to be treated.

> "Instead of putting others in their place,
> put yourself in their place."
> —John Maxwell

The other day I was in a restaurant where the waitress was obviously having a bad day. I had two ways to respond. I could write her off as weird or assume she was having a bad day and try to help. I decided to help.

I smiled at her. I said, "I'm sure looking forward to giving you a good tip today for the good service." When she brought me something, I thanked her. Her whole attitude began to change. She began to smile and relax. She couldn't do enough to see that I was served well.

> Determine that you're going to act right
> even when other people are acting wrong.

Decide that you are going to be a leader in creating good relationships by taking the right actions, even when other people are acting weird. Don't just react to them and act worse than they do. Instead, with Christ's help, practice the VIP principle. You can't really change other people, but when you keep on giving them the VIP treatment when they don't deserve it,. they will often act a little better in return. Christ calls each of us to be His representative in customer relations, the light of the world, and the salt of the earth.

This means you will have to give some thought to how you would like to be treated. That's not hard, because most of us agree on basic manners.

I Want to Be Treated Like a VIP

Study the life of Jesus and you will find He treated every person He met like someone special. No matter what their social standing was, no matter what kind of life they lived, no matter how much money they had or didn't have, they were VIPs to Jesus.

How well do you treat your employees? How well do you treat people who don't treat you like they should? How do you treat those closest to you? Do you take them for granted? Do you take advantage of them? How do you treat children? What about older people? How do you treat people who can't do anything at all to help you in your life, those who are less fortunate than you?

Scripture tells us that God is no respecter of persons; God loves every person. When Jesus came and died on the cross, He placed special value on every person alive. Scripture teaches us that the way we treat others is also the way we are treating Jesus. ". . . Whatever you did for one of the least of these brothers of mine, you did for me" (Matthew 25:40). Each person has value, so don't devalue what God prizes. Agree with God's judgment by treating each person as someone of value.

All the people I have known who have a lot of friends treat others this way. They make people feel good about themselves.

The more you create, enhance, and reinforce self-esteem in others, the more they will like you.

> Making other people feel good about themselves
> is like putting money in the bank.
> It pays rich dividends.

I Want People to Listen to Me

Everyone wants others to listen to them. Being ignored is about the worst thing that can happen to us. Most of us would rather have someone yell at us than ignore us, because a person who ignores us makes us feel like a nobody.

To get people to like you, you don't have to be a great talker. All you have to do is really listen to them. But there's a big difference between seeming to listen and really listening. Listening is really trying to understand what a person is saying. Listening involves being interested in other people and what they have to say. Scripture says it this way, "Dear brothers, don't ever forget that it is best to listen much, speak little, and not become angry" (James 1:19 TLB).

A quote from John Maxwell really spoke to me recently. It said, "A common fault as people gain more authority is a lack of patience in listening to those under them." A deaf ear is the first indication of a closed mind. The higher people go in management and the more authority they wield, the less they are forced to listen to others. Yet their need to listen is greater than ever. The farther they get from the firing line, the more they have to depend on others for correct information. If they haven't formed the habit of listening carefully and intelligently, they aren't going to get the facts they need.

Without listening, you can't succeed in your home, your business, or your relationships. The time to tune in is now. Tune out everything else and tune in to what the other person is saying.

I Want to Be Appreciated

Everyone wants to be appreciated. When companies are failing because of labor problems, it is often because employees do not feel appreciated. People will do more work for appreciation than they will for money. No one wants to be taken for granted.

> "The deepest principle in human nature
> is the craving to be appreciated."
> —William James

When you express appreciation for others, their value goes up in the way you view them and the way they view themselves. With your mate, your children, employees—anyone you relate to—when you express appreciation, you increase their value and worth. On the other hand, when you withhold appreciation, you devalue that person.

One of the best things we can do is open every conversation by expressing some kind of appreciation for the other person. That sets the tone for a positive, uplifting conversation. Everything you say from then on is built on a positive, upbeat foundation. You do want to get along well with other people, don't you? Then why not give them the words of praise and appreciation they crave?

I Want Others to Believe in Me

One of the greatest things you can do to treat others the way
you want to be treated is to believe in them. If you believe in
people, they will do almost anything to avoid disappointing
you.

In his book *Life More Abundant,* Dr. Charles Allen tells this
story:

An outcast beggar was sitting across the street from an artist's
studio. The artist saw him and quickly began to paint his
portrait. When it was finished, he called the beggar over to
look at it.

At first the beggar did not recognize himself. "Who is it?"
he kept asking. The artist smiled and said nothing. The
beggar kept looking at the portrait until recognition began to
dawn. Hesitantly he asked, "Is it me? Can it be me?"

The artist replied, "That is the man I see in you."

Then the beggar made a wonderful reply: "If that's the man
you see, that's the man I'll be."

In our world today, we always seem to try to find something
wrong with people so we can write them off or condemn them
as failures. Yet the Bible tells us, ". . . While we were still
sinners, Christ died for us" (Romans 5:8). God teaches us how
to love, to see beyond a person's past to the beautiful possibilities of what a person can become.

One of the greatest things you can do for others is to look
at them in the light of their potential, their possibilities, what
God created them to be and become.

> Build another person up by believing in him or her
> and you will become a partner in that person's
> achievements.

I Want to Be Encouraged and Edified

Do you want to be encouraged and built up? So does every other person. We live in a world that tears us down. Christ calls us to live a different way, to build other people up. We all have the opportunity to put new strength into weary hearts by lifting them up.

People who know me well know that I love chocolate. For the past couple of months, I've been watching what I eat and exercising. I am one of those people who has lost four hundred pounds—ten pounds at a time—forty different times.

The other night I was craving some chocolate-covered peanuts. I thought, *Well, I've been pretty good. I owe myself a treat.* So I went to the store and picked out a delicious-looking bag of chocolate-covered peanuts. I walked to the counter practically tasting the chocolate and peanut delicacy.

I reached in my pocket and was embarrassed to realize that although the clerk had rung up the sale, I didn't have enough money to pay for those peanuts. I started apologizing to the clerk and told her that I didn't have the money to pay for the peanuts.

Do you know what she did? She started telling me not to feel bad, that it happened to everyone sometime. Then she came over to help me find something I would like that I could afford for the one dollar I had with me. The clerk was probably in her late twenties, but she was treating me like a mother treats a child who falls down and gets a cut. Such empathy, such compassion. Instead of feeling embarrassed, I felt great!

Sometimes we do dumb things, and that is when we need encouragement the most. To be able to encourage others we need to learn how to have empathy with them, to enter into their lives and feel what they're feeling.

The next time you are hurt, instead of just thinking about yourself, try to put yourself in the other person's shoes and think and feel what he or she is experiencing. Just the act of putting yourself in another's place will actually help your own hurt.

I Want to Be Accepted

No two people are alike. If you expect other people to be just like you, you are going to be continually disappointed and at odds with others. I have one of the most wonderful, marvelous pastoral teams that any senior pastor could ever have. Yet not one of our ten pastors is like another.

The time I get in difficulty with one of the pastors is when I expect him or her to be like me. If they were like me, I wouldn't need them. I need them because they are different. They add so much richness and dimension to the ministry of our church.

Do yourself a favor and stop trying to change other people.
Do them a favor and start accepting them for the people they are.

Trying to change another person binds the relationship. Accepting other people and valuing them for who they are frees them to be the people God created them to be. It also frees you to appreciate them for who they are.

A young man whose father had been very successful in a business was asked why he did not follow in his father's steps. He explained that his father had come up the hard way and had always tried to make him tough. When the boy was growing up, his father would take him out in the yard and throw him a baseball. The boy was supposed to catch the ball ten times. However, if he caught it nine times, the father would throw the tenth pitch into the ground or high in the air, or as hard as he could throw it, just to make sure the boy missed. The boy always failed to measure up. No matter how well he did, he was never accepted by his father. His father always demanded something that the boy could not do. He set up his own son for failure.

What damage we do when we demand perfection of other people and do not accept them as they are. Jesus calls us to make winners out of people, not set them up to lose.

I Want Some Consideration and Kindness

Duke Larson tells this story: As the man and his wife returned to their seats in the dark auditorium, the husband asked the fellow seated on the aisle, "Did someone step on your feet while going out at intermission?"

"Yes, you did," he replied, expecting an apology.

"Okay, honey," the man said to his wife, "this is our row."

That's not the way to win friends and influence people. That's not the way to treat others. None of us wants to be treated like that. We do not want to be taken advantage of or taken for granted. We do not want to be treated rudely.

Kindness and consideration of others is one of the very finest ways we can express our Christian faith. The Bible says, "Be kind and compassionate to one another, forgiving each other, just as in Christ God forgave you" (Ephesians 4:32). In Colossians 3:12 we read, ". . . clothe yourselves with compassion, kindness, humility, gentleness and patience." One of the best things you can do for other people is to treat them as you want to be treated.

One of our church members expressed this bit of wisdom: "I want whatever comes out of my mouth to be sweet, because tomorrow I may have to eat it."

I Want to Be Understood

Peter Drucker, often called the father of American management, claims that 60 percent of all management problems are the result of faulty communications. Most divorces are the result of faulty communication between mates. When there are misunderstandings in human relationships, everything breaks down.

The goal of talking and listening is not to prove who's right and who's wrong, but to understand the other person's viewpoint and then decide what's best for everyone concerned.

You cannot have understanding without putting yourself in other people's places and finding out what's going on inside. What are they feeling? What are they thinking? What's their opinion? How do they see it? So many misunderstandings are avoided when we put ourselves in the other person's shoes and understand where that person is coming from. Everyone has the need to be understood. You may not agree with someone, but if you listen to him and give him the feeling that you understand, you make him feel special. Then you have a basis for working out any disagreements.

What is a wife saying when she complains, "He doesn't understand me"? What's a husband saying when he says, "She doesn't understand me"? Are they saying that they have to agree? No! They are simply saying, "Please care enough to listen. At least consider my viewpoint. Please care enough to feel what I feel." Understanding begins with putting yourself in the other person's place. Misunderstanding turns into understanding when you really start treating the other person as you want to be treated.

SEVEN

The Forgiveness Principle

**There are no lasting relationships
without forgiveness.**

Are your feelings hurt? Do you think you have been mistreated? Did you get a raw deal? If so, you have an unforgiving spirit. No matter how you try to evade it, excuse it, rationalize it, or justify it, it's there. Wherever you go, that self-destructive spirit and bad attitude go with you. This is one reality you must face: An unforgiving spirit hurts you more than anyone else. With an unforgiving spirit, you are emotionally sick. You are the loser. You are in need of powerful medicine that can heal you of what ails you. You need forgiveness.

Let's face it, forgiveness is not always easy to give. I remember a couple I married that separated after several years. The husband left home thinking the grass was greener on the other side of the fence. After five months, his beautiful young wife had pretty well accepted the situation and was readjusting.

In the meantime, his life was going from bad to worse. All the vices and loose living that had seemed so alluring were leaving him empty and lonely. He faced the cruel reality that the people he was associating with were selfish takers. They didn't care about anyone except themselves.

One night, alone in a cheap hotel room, he hit bottom. In desperation he picked up the phone, called his wife, and pleaded for help. She called me, and together we drove into a run-down section of the city to find him. The last time I had seen him he was a clean-cut, handsome young man with a lot of promise, so I was unprepared for what I saw. When he opened the door we were confronted with an unshaven, smelly, beaten man. He was so ashamed that he could not even look at us. I began to tell him how much God loved him and wanted to forgive him and give him a new beginning.

That night we knelt together and prayed the sinner's prayer. He literally wept out his sin and shame to God. When he got all straightened out with God, he looked at his wife with tears in his eyes and asked her forgiveness.

I wondered how this woman who had suffered so much would respond. She could have been bitter. But that night I witnessed a divine miracle. I watched the young couple come together in each other's arms asking for and giving forgiveness. Yes, to err is human, but to forgive is divine. And divine forgiveness opened the door for the birth of new love in their marriage. Now they are very much in love and happily married.

> **Forgiveness can set you free
> to begin again and love again.**

Jesus knew how important forgiveness is in our lives. That's why He taught us to pray, "Forgive us our trespasses as we

forgive those who trespass against us." Jesus knew that forgiveness is the only medicine that can cure an ill spirit and
restore a broken relationship.

Everyone Needs Forgiveness

Ernest Hemingway, in his short story "Capital of the World,"
tells about a father and son who lived in Spain. Their relationship had been very strained and marked by the father's
unforgiving spirit. The son had left home, and the father
didn't know where the son was.

Finally the father got to the point where he just couldn't
handle it anymore. He longed for his lost son, longed to see his
son, to tell him all was forgiven. One day he placed an ad in
the Madrid paper. This is what it said: "Dear Paco, Please
meet me in front of the newspaper office tomorrow at noon.
All is forgiven. Signed, Dad."

The next morning, eight hundred lost, homeless boys were
lined up in front of the newspaper office.

It's true that everyone needs forgiveness at some time.
Without forgiveness, our guilt binds us up and separates us
from people. Thank God for His gift of forgiveness in our
lives. Everyone also needs to give forgiveness. Peter once came
to Jesus and asked, "Lord, how many times shall I forgive my
brother when he sins against me? . . ." (Matthew 18:21).
Good question.

Jesus answered that we are to forgive seventy times seven.
That's 490 times, which is a way of saying that we are never
to stop forgiving. There is to be no limit on our forgiveness.

When we celebrated my twenty-fifth year in the ministry,
the pastoral staff and the church board gave me a custom set of
golf clubs. All my life I have played with hand-me-down
clubs. To play golf well, you need to hit the ball with the

club's "sweet spot." If you hit it there, the ball will go the farthest and the straightest. In my custom set of beautiful golf clubs, the heads of the woods and the irons have an expanded sweet spot. I can now hit the ball off center and still get good distance. I recently heard this expanded sweet spot described as being very "forgiving."

That's exactly what we need as Christians. We need to expand our "sweet spot" to be more forgiving. I can tell you one thing: The more forgiving you are, the better your life is going to be. And the more forgiving you are, the more you are going to be like Jesus.

You Cannot Afford to Be Without Forgiveness

Many people were surprised when they saw Richard Nixon sitting beside Hubert Humphrey's widow during Humphrey's televised funeral service. Supporters of Humphrey who were enemies of Nixon asked, "What's Nixon doing there?" They had been opponents for years in the Senate and then in the race for the presidency. Everyone knew how much they differed politically, and the most difficult blow Hubert Humphrey suffered was when he lost the presidency to Richard Nixon.

What happened? Why was Nixon there? Because it was Hubert Humphrey's last wish that Richard Nixon be invited to his funeral. And with the whole nation watching on television, Nixon sat by Humphrey's wife.

Forgiveness is a gift from God. It is divine and holy. When we have it, we have a right spirit within and a wholesome attitude. No matter what other people do or do not do, through forgiveness, we take the right action toward them.

Without forgiveness there are no enduring relationships If you are going to continue a healthy relationship with anyone, somewhere along the line you are going to have to forgive each other.

They had been married for thirty-two years. It should have been the happiest time in their marriage. They had made it through the struggles of raising a large family, had all the children happily married, and were financially comfortable. But with a set jaw, she poured out these words of hate: "I would rather see him dead than forgive him for what he has done with that other woman."

I said to my wounded friend, "I understand your pain and hurt. I can even see why you would be bitter. But let me tell you, unless you forgive him, you're going to go on hurting in your spirit, and there is going to be destructive bitterness between you and your husband."

True to her word, she never forgave him. Oh, they went on living together, miserably. Every day they kept destroying each other. Finally he couldn't take it anymore. His heart gave out, and he died. Following his death, she carried not only her resentment but an unbearable load of guilt mixed with hatred. How different their lives could have been if she had forgiven him.

Without forgiveness there is no emotional health and well-being
Resentment and bitterness in the spirit is like poison to the body. It will infect your thoughts, damage your emotions, and make you sick. This is why the Bible says, ". . . Watch out that no bitterness takes root among you, for as it springs up it causes deep trouble . . ." (Hebrews 12:15 TLB).

Ill feelings toward another person will make you sick, emotionally and physically. It will make you that person's slave, bound to him by your feelings.

Without forgiveness there is no saving grace in your life When

Peter asked Jesus how many times we should forgive, Jesus answered seventy times seven and then told him a parable.

There was a man who owed a huge debt; let's say he owed ten thousand dollars. The debt came due and he didn't have any money to pay it. He went to his creditor and begged him not to sell him and his wife and children and everything he had to repay the debt. The master took pity on him and cancelled the debt completely.

Then this same man who had been forgiven went out and confronted a man who owed him one hundred dollars. He grabbed the man by the throat and began to choke him. "Pay back what you owe me!" he demanded. The man who owed him fell on his knees to beg forgiveness, but the man refused and had his debtor thrown into prison.

Can you imagine? How could anyone who has been forgiven so much be unwilling to forgive another person? When the master found out what had happened, he reinstated the first man's debt and had the rascal thrown into prison. Now here's Jesus' teaching from the parable: "This is how my heavenly Father will treat each of you unless you forgive your brother from your heart" (Matthew 18:35).

> **Do you want to be forgiven?**
> **Then you must forgive others.**

If you want God's grace and forgiveness for your sins, you must forgive others their sins. If you don't forgive, there is no forgiveness for you. Quite frankly, I am glad this teaching is in the Bible. Who would want to go to heaven with people who are uptight, ill spirited, sulking, feeling sorry for themselves, choosing up sides, trying to find ways to get even, and striking back? That wouldn't be heaven; that would be hell.

And that's what happens to people who won't forgive: They live in hell on this earth.

Without forgiveness there is no new beginning   A forgiving God specializes in new beginnings. Nature doesn't forgive. Some people don't forgive. But God forgives. And He calls us to forgiveness and a new beginning.

When East Berlin was divided from West Berlin, a group of East Berliners dumped a whole truckload of garbage on the west side. The people in West Berlin could easily have retaliated, but instead they took a truckload of canned goods, bread, and milk and neatly stacked it on the East Berlin side. They put a sign on their gift that read: EACH GIVES WHAT HE HAS TO GIVE.

What do you say? To a world filled with hate, let's give love. In a world of mistakes and errors and sin, let's give forgiveness. In a world that damns people for past mistakes, let's give new beginnings.

Let the Great Forgiver Lead Your Way

Joseph, one of my favorite Old Testament characters, suffered more at the hands of abusive people than almost anyone I know, except Jesus Christ. Joseph's insanely jealous brothers sold him into slavery. If that weren't enough, once he had worked himself up into a trusted position in Potiphar's house, Potiphar's sensuous witch of a wife falsely accused Joseph. This resulted in his imprisonment for seven years. Can you imagine being in prison for seven years for something you didn't do?

Away from his family, locked in prison, the victim of cruel mistreatment and injustice, Joseph still refused to let bitterness control his life. He looked to God for healing and help in his inner spirit. Through the power of God within him, he forgave those who hadn't even asked for it.

The day came when he saw his brothers again. He could have retaliated against them when they came seeking food and help. He was now in a position of power second only to the king of Egypt. However, Joseph could hardly wait to reveal himself and extend forgiveness to his brothers. In one of the most beautiful statements in all the Bible, he said, "You intended to harm me, but God intended it for good . . ." (Genesis 50:20). Because of Joseph's forgiving heart and openly expressed forgiveness, there was complete restoration of his family. Forgiveness brought good out of what had been evil.

We all have opportunities to become bitter. We are the victims of cruel, unjust treatment we didn't deserve. Our rights are violated. Our feelings are hurt. But an unforgiving spirit is not an option for a person who wants to be everything Christ wants him to be. Look to Jesus; see Him on the cross. As He dies for your sins in your place, hear Him say, "Father, forgive them; for they know not what they do . . ." (Luke 23:34 KJV). This is forgiveness! This is Jesus! He is our forgiveness, and He is the One who shows us how to forgive.

EIGHT

The Bull's-eye Principle

Make love your number-one aim.

One morning when I woke up, this inspiring thought was in my mind: *Love is not a light that flickers and dies in the night. Love is a light that burns through the night.*

When you study our basic human needs, one stands out above all the others. We cannot live and have any sense of well-being without *love!*

I need to tell you right now that love is one of my favorite subjects. Climaxing one of the richest chapters in all the Bible, 1 Corinthians 13, Paul tells us love is the greatest thing there is. Being able to give and receive love is a greater accomplishment than anything else you could ever do.

What is love?

It is warm like the sun.
It is refreshing, like cool rain after a long drought.
It is beautiful, like roses in full bloom.
It is satisfying, like a delicious meal.

Love is the one thing no one can live well without. You need it, and I need it. The giving and receiving of love is our most urgent daily need. Without the giving and receiving of love, we are like a car with a dead battery. Jesus, who knows our every need, gave us this key commandment for our own good: "A new command I give you: Love one another. As I have loved you, so you must love one another. All men will know that you are my disciples if you love one another" (John 13:34, 35).

The Bull's-eye Principle

As the story goes, a man was driving down a country road when he saw a strange sight—arrows stuck at random in the side of a large barn. A man was up on a ladder, painting targets around the arrows so that each arrow was centered in the bull's-eye of the target.

When the observer asked the farmer what was going on, the farmer laughed. "Oh, that's the village idiot. He's taken up archery, and he likes to think he's hitting the bull's-eye."

What is the bull's-eye principle? It is my summation of the great love chapter that Paul gave to us in 1 Corinthians 13:

Make love your number-one aim.

So many people in our lives need love. I was startled to read of some research that shows 90 percent of divorces are initiated by women. What's the problem? The problem is that women do not feel loved by their husbands. But the man responds, "I work hard at a job and provide for my family. I'm home nights. Sometimes I help with the kids. What more does she want?"

Any wife can tell you that she needs affection from her husband. She needs him to listen. She needs him to understand what she's feeling and thinking and to affirm her as being the most important person in his life.

Women need nonsexual love. An attractive, young, successful single woman committed suicide. In the business world she was a success, but in her personal life she was hurting. She slept with many men trying to find love. In her diary were these words: "Where are the men with the flowers and music? Where are the men who call and ask for genuine, actual dates? Where are the men who would like to share more than my bed, my booze, my food? I would like to have in my life, once, the kind of sexual relationship which is a part of a loving relationship." She never did.

Without God's kind of love, men and women perish from a variety of diseases of mind, body, and soul.

The good news is: God is love, and His love is revealed to us and given to us in Jesus' coming to this earth and dying on the cross for us. While we were still sinners, Christ died for us!

There is no need for you to go without love. Receive the warming, healing, lifting, changing, fulfilling love of God in Christ. The most important thing for you to do is to receive God's love and give it to others.

We live in a world of mixed-up priorities, and it's easy for us to get our priorities mixed-up, too. But there is no substitute for love. Whatever you accomplish or achieve, nothing will take the place of love. Your life will never be in order unless you make love your top priority. Nothing in this whole world can take the place of love.

Relate to Others Out of Love, Not Fear

How do you relate to people? Do you relate to them out of love or out of fear? You need to know that fear destroys love and love overcomes and conquers fear. In 2 Timothy 1:7 (KJV), we read these words: "For God hath not given us the spirit of fear; but of power, and of love, and of a sound mind."

What kind of messages do you send out to other people? What kind of vibrations? Do you know that you send different chemical messages through your body and communicate these messages to others? These messages are communicated both verbally and nonverbally.

A woman who has spent her life training nurses expressed a profound concept when she said, "When I train nurses, I tell them to be nutritious people; don't be toxic people." She went on to explain. "We have some nurses in our hospital who impart fear wherever they go. They are toxic people. When they go into a room, they infect that patient with the poison of fear, negative feelings, and doubt. On the other hand, we have nurses who are very nutritious persons. Everywhere they go, the way they talk and touch and listen expresses love that builds up and gives nutrition to the patient. They become agents of God's healing."

You can send two basic types of messages to other people. The first message is called syntonic. This is a warm message of love. It sends positive hormones throughout your whole body and creates health and well-being. As you relay this message to others, it brings health and well-being into their lives.

The second kind of message is called catatoxic. This is the war message, the message of fear. "Fight, destroy, get even," it says. "Don't ever let your guard down." This sends the message of stress throughout your whole body and makes you at war with everyone you meet.

Stop allowing fear to destroy your relationships.

When you start to feel the fear of rejection, counteract it with the fact that God loves you and accepts you just as you are. Be warmed by the love of God in your life. If someone doesn't accept you, that's okay. You are already a loved person, and because you are loved, you can give love to others.

Some people are actually afraid to love because they don't want to risk being hurt. They pull back in a shell, saying, "I'll never love again." That's the dumbest thing you can do. When you do that, you go on hurting, hurting, hurting. Stand up to that fear. The way to be healed of that pain is to love again, even more than before.

Some people are afraid of success. As they become more successful, they start getting uptight because they are moving out of their comfort zone. The answer is to grow in God's love and enlarge the concept you have of yourself. Yes, God has given us a wonderful gift. He has not given us the spirit of fear but of love and of power and of a sound mind. Stand up and choose love over fear.

In 1 John 4:18 we read these profound words: ". . . perfect love drives out fear. . . ."

Love Is Something You Do

Whoever said it was easy to love? Is it easy to love

- a person who mistreats one of your children?

- someone who is trying to prove you wrong and himself right?
- a person who is rude and abusive to you?
- a person who takes advantage of you in a business deal?
- a person who is ignoring or slighting you?

What about that person at the shopping center who pulls into a parking space you've been waiting for? What about the person who disagrees with you?

Love is the name of the Christian game. "Dear friends, let us practice loving each other, for love comes from God and those who are loving and kind show that they are the children of God, and that they are getting to know him better. But if a person isn't loving and kind, it shows that he doesn't know God—for God is love" (1 John 4:7, 8 TLB). Love is the proof of a Christian pudding. If you say you are a Christian, then act like one by putting love into practice.

According to the Bible, love is something you do.

- Regardless of how inconvenient it is
- Regardless of what others do
- Regardless of how you feel
- When it comes to love, action does speak louder than words.

Jesus is our example. Look at how He treated Judas. Judas was one of His chosen twelve disciples. Jesus confided in, trusted, and trained Judas. Yet Judas turned against Jesus and betrayed Him for thirty pieces of silver.

On that last night at the Lord's Supper, knowing full well what Judas had already done, knowing that he would give Him the kiss of betrayal before the night was over, Jesus chose to show Judas the same kind of love He showed the other eleven. As He went from disciple to disciple, He tenderly and compassionately washed their feet and expressed His love for them. When He came to Judas, He gave him the same un-conditional heartfelt love. Jesus did not change the way He acted or lived because someone chose to turn against Him.

Love is something we do because it is the right thing to do. It is the way of our Lord Jesus. And when we don't have it within us, we need to pray and pray until we are empowered by the Holy Spirit with His love.

In Romans 5:5 we have this promise: ". . . God has poured out his love into our hearts by the Holy Spirit, whom he has given us." When you allow the Holy Spirit to work through your life, you will have no shortage of love. Love will flow in abundance through your life.

Love is not an option; it is a must!

The Time to Love Is Now

Dr. Charles Allen, in his book *The Miracle of Love,* tells of this experience.

I talked to a mother just recently whose teen-age daughter is in trouble. She's not married, and she is going to have a baby.

The mother said many harsh, bitter things about her. Her mother talked about the family being disgraced. I finally said to that mother, "Stop saying all those bitter things. That girl is hurt enough. You go home and tell that girl and you tell her many times every day that you love her, and that you are standing by her, that you are going to help her all the way through." I told that mother, "If you do not love your daugh-ter now, she will likely never need your love again."

The time to love those who are walking through the darkness of the night is now! Remember, love is not something that flickers and dies in the night. Love burns through until the day, and the darker the night, the brighter love will shine.

The one goal that I have set for myself in life above all other goals is the one I want you to make the top priority of your life.

Let love be your greatest aim.

NINE

The Mr. and Mrs. Principle

"Honor Christ by submitting to each other"
(Ephesians 5:21 TLB).

What is the Mr. and Mrs. principle? Making your marriage
really successful. Everyone wants a successful marriage. In
Ecclesiastes 9:9 (TLB) we read these exciting words: "Live happily with the woman you love through the fleeting days of life,
for the wife God gives you is your best reward down here for
all your earthly toil."

Someone once asked me, "Pastor, how would you define a
successful marriage?" It's interesting that the Bible defines
marriage as the very thing that everyone who's married desires.
When God created male and female and brought them together in the bond of marriage, He said, "For this reason a
man will leave his father and mother and be united to his wife,
and they will become one flesh" (Genesis 2:24). The next verse
describes how they celebrated their oneness. "The man and his
wife were both naked, and they felt no shame" (Genesis 2:25).

It is God's perfect plan that a husband and wife come

together as one, physically, emotionally, and spiritually. They are to share intimacy. When a married couple achieves this, it is ecstasy. No other relationship can climb to a summit like this one. In order to make your marriage really successful and to experience that wonderful feeling of oneness, do the following seven things.

Make a Total Commitment From Your Heart

To have a successful life, one must pay a price. In no area of life is this more true than in marriage. To have a successful marriage, you have to pay a price. You must give up some things and devote yourself diligently to other things.

People don't get married and just live happily ever after. That's a fairy tale. Most of us are familiar with these words in the marriage vows: "For better for worse, for richer for poorer, in sickness and in health, to love and to cherish, till death us do part." Most people who get married have no understanding of what those words really mean. But for a marriage to be successful, you have to learn what they mean and put them into practice.

The first thing required to make your marriage really successful is summed up in one word: commitment. Genesis says that in order to become one flesh, we have to "leave and cleave." What does that mean? It means committing yourself to marriage as the primary relationship of your life. When you have done this, every other relationship becomes secondary: job, children, education, sports, and everything else.

What's in your heart today? Is there a will to make your marriage the best it can be? Or is there selfishness that says, "Well, if it doesn't work out, I'll just throw in the towel."

A good marriage has to begin in the heart. Is your heart right? Does your heart hold love, submission, cooperation, wanting to be on the same team, forgiveness, edification, seeing the best in the other person? Open your heart to God and let Him create the right heart and spirit within you toward your mate and your marriage. God wants to help you in your marriage. But He can't do much with a rebellious heart or one that clings to ill feelings or decides to do its own thing. You'll never have a close marriage and oneness until you make a total commitment of your heart to God, your mate, and your marriage.

Understand His or Her Needs and Meet Them

The second thing you can do to foster oneness in your marriage is to become aware of each other's needs and learn to meet them. If you will do this, you will affair-proof your marriage. More than that, you will have taken a big step toward making your marriage close, intimate, and growing.

Repeatedly in my pastoral counseling, I see serious rifts between husbands and wives who do not know that males and females have very different sexual drives. Not understanding this, they get into a negative cycle where neither meets the other's needs.

The wife says, "He doesn't love me. He doesn't understand me. He doesn't even begin to meet my emotional needs. All he ever wants is my body. He's an animal."

The husband's side of the story is, "Look, I work my fool head off supporting that woman and our kids. What more does she want from me?" The upset husband continues, "She never has time for me. Her mind is always occupied with the children or something else. It is a terrible thing to feel rejected."

The wife responds, "I cook for him, I iron his clothes, make his bed, do his laundry, take care of his kids, work at a job to help support this family. What more does he want?"

I can't tell you how many times I've seen this negative cycle repeated in the lives of good people who once really loved each other. Who's right and who's wrong? Both are right and both are wrong. Neither one really understands that males and females differ. Because of the variation in psychological and physical drives, men and women hold very different viewpoints.

The female naturally focuses on her nesting and maternal activities. She has an enormous need to feel secure. She looks to her husband to meet her emotional needs by caring enough to listen to her and accept her. When the wife's emotional needs are met—and only then—she becomes responsive sexually.

On the other hand, the male's reproductive drive centers on sex. A wife can do everything else for him, but unless she's responsive to his sexual advances, he's going to feel rejected, wounded, and unloved. As you might know from firsthand experience, all kinds of misunderstandings arise because the male approaches the female from his viewpoint while the female approaches the male from her viewpoint.

What's the solution? It is to see that we are different and to put ourselves in the other person's shoes. His needs are not her needs, and her needs are not his needs.

Remember, the Bible teaches us to give first and then we will receive. One characteristic of followers of Christ is that they are givers, not selfish takers. Gain oneness in your marriage by finding out what your mate's needs are and meeting them.

Work at Growing Together

In his book *His Needs, Her Needs,* Willard Harley has likened marriage to a love bank. If you keep making withdrawals without putting deposits into your bank, you'll go bankrupt. You got married in the first place because your account in the love bank became substantial and you liked it.

Let me ask you a couple of questions. How much time did you spend together in conversation when you were courting? If you were like I was, it didn't matter that I had a full-time job and many other responsibilities. I found a way to be with Margi and talk to her for hours every day. When we were courting, even if it meant going without sleep, we would find the time to be together and talk, making deposits in the love bank.

How much time a day do you now spend talking with your mate? All too many couples spend less than ten minutes a day talking to each other. Some don't really talk at all. If you don't spend time talking to each other, you're going to drift apart. You have to plan time every day to be together and talk. If you do that, you will grow together. If you don't, you will grow apart. Spending time in conversation will draw you together, and you will become best friends.

My wife, Margi, and I are best friends because we spend a great deal of time every day in conversation. We talk and listen and share life together.

Many couples develop separate interests as life goes on. Pretty soon they are going in different directions all of the time, which is a sure way to grow apart. It's all right for you to have separate interests, but if you are smart, you will also have overlapping interests you both share. The more interests and activities you share, the more you'll grow together. When a husband and wife are going in different directions following their own interests, the marriage may survive, but it certainly is not going to have oneness and closeness.

Having overlapping interests means that you have to do some things that may not be exactly what you would choose on your own. For example, I don't really enjoy shopping all that much. But there are times when I'll go shopping with Margi, not because I want to shop, but because I want to be with her.

I recently heard a glowing testimony of oneness from a couple who started walking together every morning and playing golf together once a week. They are having a great time. Are you growing together? If so, wonderful! Are you growing apart? If so, what are you going to do about it? The time to do something about it is now, before it's too late.

Talk Out Conflict and Compromise

In a good marriage there is going to be some conflict. No two people who are alive and healthy and expressive are always going to have the same viewpoint. As a pastor I worry a whole lot more about people who don't talk than about those who have some conflict.

However, it is important how we work through and work out our conflicts. Conflict can either be destructive or constructive. It becomes destructive when you start trying to prove who's right and who's wrong, start dragging up the past and using it like an ax, or start using "you" messages and accusing or blaming.

When is conflict good? When it leaves room for each individual to express himself or herself openly and completely, with the other person listening.

> To reveal is better than to conceal.

Two heads are better than one. Two people see twice as much as one person. No one has all the facts or all the answers. What an asset to have two viewpoints! The Bible teaches us there is great strength in getting different vantage points, since we all have limitations and blind spots.

When you've talked it all out and listened to each other's viewpoint, then make the compromise. Do what's best for everyone concerned. Remember that compromise is not a sign of weakness. It is a sign of strength, because having the right spirit and the right attitude is so much more important than being right on some issue. Work as a team, make the compromise, and stick with it.

Help Your Mate to Grow

At my men's TLC breakfast on Friday morning recently, one of our men described his personal goal of helping his wife maximize her abilities as a person. Instead of trying to hold her back or dominate her, he was encouraging her to be everything God had created her to be. I thought that was terrific. I said to myself, "Now there is a man who knows how to love a woman!"

Pay Close Attention to the Spirit of Your Marriage

In the previous chapter, I said that there are no enduring relationships without forgiveness. Certainly, there are no enduring marriages without forgiveness.

As you live together in the closeness of marriage, it is inevitable that in some careless, unguarded moment you are going to hurt the other person's feelings. When the spirit of your mate is wounded, your marriage is wounded. Have you had the experience where things are just not right at home, the atmosphere is tense, and maybe no one's talking? When I have wounded Margi's spirit, I know it. When you have wounded your mate's spirit, you'll know it, too. There's anger and hurt in the atmosphere. As one man told me, "When my wife wore a coat to bed, I knew I was in trouble."

The longer you let this go on, the worse it gets. The Bible says, ". . . Do not let the sun go down while you are still angry" (Ephesians 4:26). In other words, take care of dissension quickly in your marriage.

The only way to heal a wounded spirit is to confess what you have done wrong and ask for forgiveness. If you don't know what you've done, then ask your mate how you have hurt her feelings. Get it out in the open. Talk about it. Ask for and give forgiveness. Your marriage needs it. Besides, making up can be so much fun!

Let the Holy Spirit Teach You

When it comes to learning how to love each other, we need help. Jesus sent the Holy Spirit to teach us how to apply the love of God in our lives.

Ed Wheat, in his book *Love Life,* points out the five kinds of love we need in our marriages. We need physical love, romantic love, friendship love, family love or belonging, and agape love. Agape love is the deep spiritual love that meets our deepest needs. It's a love that loves unconditionally and completely, the way God loves us.

To have complete oneness in a marriage, we must surrender to the Holy Spirit first and then to our mates. We must give up competition and choose cooperation. We must give up rebellion for submission. We must give up demanding our own way in favor of a life of serving the other person.

In the context of talking about our need to be filled with the Holy Spirit, Paul writes, "Submit to one another out of reverence for Christ" (Ephesians 5:21).

Yield yourself in your marriage to the Holy Spirit. Let the

Holy Spirit cleanse you from anything in your marriage that is not pleasing to God. Reject anything that does not make for oneness. Then let the Holy Spirit bring the love of God flowing through you and your relationship. In the power of the Spirit, choose and cultivate all five of the loves you need in your married life.

PART THREE

*Multiply
What's Been Given
to You*

TEN
The Manager Principle

Before you can manage others, you must manage yourself.

Some who will read these words manage many people. Others don't employ or manage anybody and may wonder what this chapter has to do with them. The truth is, everyone is a manager. The only question is, what kind of manager are you going to be?

- Responsible or irresponsible?
- Faithful or unfaithful?
- Successful or unsuccessful?

The choice is yours! One thing I have learned from Scripture and from practical experience is this: People cannot be successful in their own businesses until they can be successful in working for others. In other words, if you can't get along with the boss and the people you're working with, becoming the boss won't help you get along any better. If you can't manage yourself well enough to work successfully for another person, you certainly can't manage yourself and supervise others.

The Bible word for a manager is *steward*. The biblical concept of stewardship relates to managing our lives in a way that gives glory and honor to God. Someone has said it this way:

> "Our life is a gift from God,
> what we do with our life is our gift back to God.
> The giving of that life back to God
> is our stewardship."

Jesus used a parable to teach us what it means to be a good, successful manager and what it is to be an unfaithful steward or miserable manager (*see* Matthew 25:14–30). In the parable, there are three servants. The master entrusted each of them with some of his property. To the first he gave five portions, to the second he gave two portions, and to the last he gave one portion.

The one with five portions and the one with two portions put their assets to work. They gave it everything they had. They were responsible with what they had been given. When it came time for the accounting, they brought back not only what they had been given but a great increase because of their responsible and faithful management.

The third manager decided that he hadn't been given very much. He lived in rebellion. He wasted his life. He buried his talents. He surrendered his life to negative thinking and didn't do anything. To be an unfaithful, poor manager, all you have to do is nothing. When he came before the master, what he had been given was taken away from him because he had mismanaged it. He was judged unfaithful and cast out.

From this parable we learn that each of us is a manager. We are accountable to God for what we do with our potential. The greatest possible success is not to outdo someone else but to be faithful in managing what we have been given. The worst possible failure is to be found unfaithful in managing our lives and resources.

Here is an awesome thought:
You are accountable to God for
everything in your life.

Get It Straight Who the Boss Is

You can never be successful in your work until you learn to take orders from the boss. No matter where you work, you are going to have a boss. If you go into business for yourself, one thing you are going to find out is that you still have bosses. You go to borrow money at the bank for your business and you have bosses. You go to purchase machinery and you have bosses. Income tax time comes around and you have bosses. You need to please customers and they are bosses.

Let's come at this a little different way. Let me ask you a question. Do you own your home? If so, who owned the property your house is on before you were alive? Who owned the property 2,000 years ago? Who is going to own the property after you're dead? To whom does your mate belong? Every time I start to act like I own Margi, I cause conflict in our relationship. As long as we don't try to own each other, we get along beautifully.

Who owns your children? Do you own them, or are they a treasure and gift from God, placed in your care for a period of time? Who owns your paycheck? Is it all yours to spend however you want? Or is it something God has entrusted you to manage for His glory?

Who owns your body? Scripture tells us that our body is the temple of the living God. We're not our own. We have been bought for a price—the price of Jesus' blood to forgive our sins, cleanse and restore us, and give us worth and dignity as children of God.

This week I asked myself what I owned. The Holy Spirit brought Psalm 24:1, 2 to mind: "The earth is the Lord's, and everything in it, the world, and all who live in it; for he founded it upon the seas and established it upon the waters."

Get it straight: God owns it all.

The first step in becoming a successful manager of your life is to know that God owns it all. You begin to show wisdom on the day you recognize Him as Lord of all. "Every good and perfect gift cometh from above . . ." (*see* James 1:17). Everything that I am and everything that I have is a gift—a trust—from God.

"The greatest thing is to be found at one's post as a child of God, living each day as though it were our last, but planning as though our world might last a hundred years" (C. S. Lewis).

Win by Making Others Winners

A while back I was reading an article by an expert on productivity. For years, he had studied what companies can do to increase their productivity. His conclusion was what he called the triple win. The triple win occurs when customers win, employees win, and the company wins. When all three entities benefit from what's being done, productivity will sail to an all-time high.

The expert pointed out that some companies center on the customer but forget about their employees. The employees become unhappy and customer service dries up. A company wins by making others winners. You give the customer a good product and value. You treat your employees as you want to be treated. Then you prosper and everybody ends up winning.

Do you know what a good real estate deal is? It is when everyone wins, when it's a good deal for everyone involved. That is contrary to the way a lot of people think. They think if they can take advantage of another person and cut a fat deal for themselves, that's a good deal. That is not a good deal. If it's a bad deal for the other person, it will come back to haunt you. A good deal is good for everyone.

In any business or management situation, people are the greatest asset. When people are encouraged and built up, the best is brought out in them. They become successful.

When it comes to being a good steward, how we treat other people is important. Jesus told us to treat others as we want to be treated. The Scriptures teach us that a part of our accountability to God is how we have treated others. In business, your greatest asset is the people who work for you.

Be Responsible

I have observed over the years that whether it's in the Boy Scouts, a ball team, the church, or a business, the person who behaves responsibly rises, like cream, to the top.

What does it mean to be a responsible person? It is the opposite of being irresponsible.

Without responsibility, life quickly deteriorates. Psychiatrists say that one of the biggest steps in rehabilitating people mentally and emotionally is to get them to the point where they become responsible. We must stop blaming other people and take the responsibility for ourselves and for what's going on in our lives.

When it comes to our Christian service, nothing is more important than personal responsibility. As we read in 1 Corinthians 15:58 (KJV), ". . . be ye stedfast, unmoveable, always abounding in the work of the Lord. . . ."

To be a successful manager or steward in God's sight, you do not always have to be successful. You do have to be faithful and keep on doing what God has given you to do.

When Margi and I were vacationing in Hawaii, Margi was doing some laundry and met a teenage girl who looked about thirteen but said she was fifteen. She was a high school dropout, a church dropout, and in many ways a society dropout. She was doing laundry for five construction workers. She was living with one of them without marriage or commitment and was being used as a slave and plaything.

In our society there is a lot of dropping out. Every time we see someone drop out, we should pray for him or her. We should also draw closer to God and be thankful to Him for the opportunities of service and ministry He has given us. "Be stedfast, unmoveable, always abounding in the work of the Lord." The way to win is to keep on trucking, keep on doing what is right.

How to Manage Success

> For some, success is harder
> to manage than to obtain.

Through diligence and dedication, many people have climbed their particular mountain to a pinnacle of success, only to forget what got them there and fall off the cliff down the mountainside.

Should Christians strive for success? Let's ask the question another way. Does failure bless anybody? Does failure bring out our best? Does failure glorify our Father in heaven? Obviously the answer is no, especially when we remember that we defined success this way: Success is being the best person you can be to the glory of God.

When you're faithful in developing and using your talents to God's glory, there comes an increase. God has written a law of increase into the very nature of our universe. When you sow good seeds and cultivate them, you reap a harvest with benefits. Then the question becomes: How are you going to manage this increase?

The Bible says, ". . . Much is required from those to whom much is given, for their responsibility is greater" (Luke 12:48 TLB). Here are some suggestions on how to manage success to the glory of God:

- Stay dependent on the Lord.
- Don't get the big head.
- Keep doing the things that got you there in the first place.
- Don't change the product.
- In your walk with Jesus, keep adjusting your self-concept and self-talk to be comfortable with who you are now and what God is doing through your life.
- Help other people be successful. The more of your success you give away, the more it will multiply.

ELEVEN
The Andrew Principle

Only what we share multiplies.

Right now I want to take you on an adventure to an exciting place. At this place, which is mentioned in all four New Testament Gospels, we are going to witness a miracle. You are going to see before your very eyes this truth: Sharing works miracles.

In John 6 we read that Jesus crossed to the far shore of the Sea of Galilee, a great crowd with enormous needs following Him. He went up the hillside and sat down, and they gathered around Him, all five thousand men. Add the children and the women, and there were approximately twenty thousand people gathered around Jesus on the hillside.

What a teacher Jesus was! The crowd sat there spellbound, listening all day to this One who taught with such clarity and authority. Then as evening approached, the people became very hungry because they had not brought any provisions with them. This was a giant problem: twenty thousand hungry people and no food.

Jesus called one of His disciples, Philip, and asked how they were going to feed the multitude. Philip, an impossibility thinker, responded with all the reasons they couldn't do it.

"We aren't in downtown Jerusalem; we are out here in the wilderness. There isn't any place to buy food. Even if there were a place, we don't have nearly enough money to buy food for this multitude." Philip could see only the reasons why it couldn't be done. To the person who has no faith, meeting needs is always impossible.

Then Jesus turned to another disciple, Andrew. Andrew was quite a man. He was not a natural leader, but he was always looking for the possibility, believing that somehow the need could be met. Andrew was the son of Jonah, the brother of Simon Peter, and one of the first disciples. He had left everything to follow Jesus. Andrew, looking for a possibility, found a boy with the equivalent of five Twinkies and two sardines. That didn't look like very much. In fact, it didn't look like anything, considering the need.

Of course, to the boy, it was everything. It was all his lunch, and growing boys sure do get hungry. If you were this little boy and you were famished and someone asked you to give your lunch to a huge crowd, what would you do? The boy, although young, made the right choice. He was a whole lot smarter than some adults. He wouldn't hold back something Jesus wanted from him. He responded and gave the Master what he had. And what he gave became the seed for a great miracle.

Jesus, the miracle worker, the Son of God, took the loaves and the fishes, gave thanks, blessed them, and began to distribute them. As He did, the most marvelous miracle happened. The food kept multiplying and multiplying, and multiplying, until the entire twenty thousand were fed and blessed by the miracle. Then there were twelve baskets of food left over.

> Stingy people will never
> see the miracles of God;
> generous people will
> see the miracles of God.

Sharing Is the Only Way to Win Others to Christ

In John 1:41 we read, "The first thing Andrew did was to find his brother Simon and tell him, 'We have found the Messiah' (that is, the Christ)." As soon as Andrew found Jesus Christ personally, he ran and introduced his brother to Jesus.

> Finding Christ is the greatest thing
> that can ever happen in your life.
> Bringing another to Christ is the greatest thing
> you can do for another person.

Andrew was a personal soul winner. As I said before, he was not a natural leader. But his brother, Peter, was the one who preached on the day of Pentecost, when three thousand converts were added to the Church. Where would Peter have been without his brother? Peter might never have found Jesus if Andrew had not introduced them.

Our brothers and sisters, our co-workers, our neighbors, our acquaintances may never know Jesus if we don't personally take the initiative and put forth the effort to introduce them to Him. The greatest thing you can do for another person is to introduce him or her to Jesus.

Since I was fifteen, my passion has been souls. That passion still burns brightly today. I look across the great city where I live and feel the pain and the cries of people who need my Savior. How can I do less than give them the best—Jesus!

Any Christian can lead someone else to Jesus. Recently my mother turned eighty-three. Just about a year ago, she moved out of her own home and into a retirement center. It was a big adjustment, but I know she's no longer lonely, because she enjoys being around people.

The other night I was talking with her on the phone. She was so excited. A boy in his senior year of high school, who used to deliver her paper, had come to the home for a visit. My mom saw him, began to talk to him, and realized that he was really down. She invited him to her apartment and had the great joy of leading this young man to know Jesus Christ personally.

There's no greater joy than to share Christ with someone else. Every time you share Christ with someone else, it's like experiencing it fresh and new all over again for yourself.

Sharing Is the Only Way to Multiply Love

Can you ever get too much love? Every one of us can use more love. Do you know how to get more love?

You don't get love by pulling back into a shell and separating yourself from other people. You don't get love by being a critical person, by picking at another person's faults. You don't get love by being ugly and harsh or by sitting around and expecting people to come wash your feet. Love is like a magic penny: If you give it away, you end up having more.

Love is one thing you lose if you don't share it. But the more you share it and give it away, the more it multiplies.

Sharing Is the Only Way to
Keep From Being Selfish

Do you know what is public enemy number one in our society? It acts like a giant wrecking ball in marriages. It makes people who seem to have almost everything unhappy. This problem has been with us since the Garden of Eden. It works mischief in each of our lives. It is a problem that will bring destruction to your life if you don't deal with it.

The problem is selfishness. "I want what I want when I want it! And I don't care what others want." This is humanity at its lowest point.

When will we learn that the more we try to keep something, the more we lose it? The more we try to hoard something, the more it turns rotten in our hands.

There are two contrasting bodies of water in Palestine. One is alive and the other is dead. One breathes with fish and plant life, while in the other, nothing can live. The Sea of Galilee is a beautiful lake, while the Dead Sea is almost totally lifeless. What makes the difference?

The Sea of Galilee not only takes in water but gives it to the Jordan River. The water of that famous river turns the dry desert into a gorgeous garden. In its giving, it blesses and multiplies. On the other hand, the Dead Sea has no outlet. It gives nothing and remains dead.

This is an eternal principle of life. We call it the Andrew principle: Only what we share multiplies.

Sharing Is the Way to Gain Ego Satisfaction

Recently I received something in the mail that made me feel so good, so proud, so satisfied. It was a lay pastor training manual from the First Church of God in Wichita, Kansas. The pastor there is a friend who has visited our Northwest Church Growth Institute, as have church leaders from many other places.

We tell our guests to take our training manual—which we spent years putting together in the school of hard knocks and which is filled with principles and ideas that work— copy it, and use it all they want. As long as they don't sell it to others, it's theirs to use. We freely share this material. As a result, we've had sample training manuals come back to us that were copied so directly they even had some of our original misspellings.

When I got this training manual, I saw it had everything from ours that needed to be there. It also had a couple of pages of material that we hadn't thought of. No father could be prouder of a child than I felt when I saw and read what my friend had reproduced and was using in his church.

You gain ego satisfaction through sharing whatever you have with others. When you give something away, it just keeps multiplying.

It is never easy to visit a person who is terminally ill. A few years ago I went to the hospital to visit one of our members who was dying of cancer. We had become very close through her illness and had shared both laughter and tears.

This time when I walked into her room, her lips quivered and her eyes filled with tears. "Dale," she barely whispered, "I'm so glad you're here." I took her weakened, withered hands and held them in mine as we talked together about heaven and what it was going to be like to see Jesus. Then together we fellowshiped with Him in prayer. It was one of the most holy moments.

As I was leaving, I asked, "Is there anything that I can do for you?"

Her last words were, "Just keep on loving me." I assured

her that I would stand by her and would soon be back to see
her. As I left, I had a sense of sadness, but I also had a sense
of fulfillment. You see, as I gave her love, I received love. As
I gave her comfort, I received comfort.

Sharing Is the Only Way to Keep the Miracle Going

In our Bible story we saw twenty thousand hungry people
whose needs were met in a wonderful way. But what would
have happened if the little boy had refused to share? What if
he had said, "I am going to keep my lunch"?

I have a deep concern. It is easy for people who have been
blessed to take things for granted. If we do that and stop
sharing, we will stop the blessings of God on our churches, our
lives, and our families.

Do you know that when you bring your tithes into the
storehouse, you are sharing? When you invite your friends to
church, you are sharing. When you reach out in concern and
love with words of encouragement to another person, you are
sharing. When you give of yourself in service and ministry to
others in Jesus' name, you are sharing.

> Remember, only what we share multiplies.
> What we hold back will be lost.
> Jesus said, "If you give, you will receive."

Sharing Is Being Responsible to the Holy Spirit

A little girl is kneeling beside her bed. She says, "Dear God,
if You're there and You hear my prayer, could You please just
touch me?" Just then she feels a touch. She gets so excited! She
says, "Thank You, thank You, God, for touching me!"

Then she looks up, sees her older sister, and gets a little suspicious. "Did you touch me?"

The sister answers, "Yes, I did."

"What did you do that for?"

"God told me to."

The Christian life is an adventure when you are in fellowship with the Holy Spirit and you flow with Him. When He tells you to share by speaking a word, you speak a word. When He tells you to share of your resources, you share of your resources. When He tells you to share of your life and ministry with others, you say, "Yes, Lord." When He tells you to pray for someone, you pray.

The Church of Jesus Christ has the greatest administrator in all the world, the Holy Spirit. As we respond to Him and say, "Yes, Lord," and as we share, the miracle will go on and on.

TWELVE

The Blessing Principle

A tithing person is a blessed person; a tithing church is a blessed church.

- Do you need more money?
- Do you want God's abundance and blessing in your life?
- Do you want to be a partner with God in doing great things on this earth?
- Do you want to experience the joy of giving?
- Then it is essential that you put into practice the blessing principle.

The blessing principle involves tithing and is expressed in Malachi 3:10: " 'Bring the whole tithe into the storehouse, that there may be food in my house. Test me in this,' says the Lord Almighty, 'and see if I will not throw open the floodgates of heaven and pour out so much blessing that you will not have room enough for it.' "

When you give God the first tenth of your income, you can claim this blessing that He will open the floodgates of heaven and pour out so much blessing that you will not have room for it.

Tithing begins with making a personal blessing-pact covenant with God. In Genesis 28 we read about Jacob's fascinat-
ing dream at Bethel. Jacob was in dire need. He was away
from home and hated by his brother Esau, whom he had
deceived. Somewhere out there in the wilderness between
Beersheba and Haran, Jacob stopped for the night.

In his restless sleep, Jacob dreamed of a stairway resting on
the earth with its top reaching to heaven and God's angels
ascending and descending. You might say he got a true vision
of steps to success.

In his vision, Jacob saw God as a provider of unlimited
resources. He received the promise of prosperity in these words
(Genesis 28:13,14):

". . . I am the Lord, the God of your father Abraham and the
God of Isaac. I will give you and your descendants the land on
which you are lying. Your descendants will be like the dust of
the earth, and you will spread out to the west and to the east,
to the north and to the south. All peoples on earth will be
blessed through you and your offspring."

Then God's promise to Jacob continued: "I am with you and
will watch over you wherever you go, and I will bring you
back to this land. I will not leave you until I have done what
I have promised you" (v. 15).

The very first thing the next morning, Jacob arose and made
a blessing-pact covenant with God. This was the vow that
Jacob made with God (vv. 20–22): ". . . If God will be with
me and will watch over me on this journey I am taking and
will give me food to eat and clothes to wear so that I return
safely to my father's house, then the Lord will be my God. This
stone that I have set up as a pillar will be God's house, and of
all that you give me I will give you a tenth."

This blessing-pact was a personal agreement between Jacob and God that for the rest of his life, Jacob would give the first tenth of all his income to God. Jacob kept this promise all the days of his life, and God blessed him with overflowing material and spiritual abundance.

I believe that God Almighty, who has created everything on our earth and above our earth and beyond our earth, who knows no limits, only abundance, wants to pour out blessings in your life and mine.

> Those who enter into a blessing-pact
> covenant with God are blessed by God.

God Becomes Your Provider

Where did tithing begin? Tithing was given to us before the Ten Commandments. Abraham was the first one to make a blessing covenant with God and give a tenth of his income as a tithe, and Abraham discovered that God was an abundant provider. Abraham came to know God as JEHOVAH JIREH, meaning God, my Provider. Abraham actually became one of the most wealthy and prosperous men of ancient times.

That does not mean that Abraham did not go through times of stress and testing. Abraham waited twenty-five long years before he received his promised son, Isaac. He was well past ninety years of age, and Isaac was his fondest dream come true. Oh, how he loved his miracle son, Isaac.

Then came another severe time of testing. God told him to take his son on a journey to Mt. Moriah and offer him up as a sacrifice to the Lord. Please understand that in the ancient world, pagan people often made human sacrifice to gods.

Abraham knew JEHOVAH JIREH was a loving and providing heavenly Father. He didn't understand what was being asked of him. But, in faith and obedience, he did this most difficult thing. He took his son and made the long, difficult climb to the top of Mt. Moriah. Along the way his son said, . . . "The fire and wood are here, . . . but where is the lamb for the burnt offering?" (Genesis 22:7). Can you imagine what pain went through Abraham's heart when his son asked that question? Nevertheless, Abraham determined that he would trust the God who had never failed him. Somehow, some way, God would provide for his need. (Only people who put God first in money matters by tithing can have the kind of faith and obedience that Abraham had when the tough times come.)

After arriving at the top of the mountain, Abraham prepared the altar, arranged the wood, and with a heart that was tearing apart, bound his son. Can you imagine the emotion both father and son were feeling at that moment?

In total obedience to JEHOVAH JIREH, Abraham placed his son of promise on the altar and raised the knife to slay him. Just as he was about to bring the knife down through the heart of his son, he heard a magnificent voice from heaven saying, "Abraham, Abraham, don't harm your son. Now I know that you are obedient to my command" (*see* Genesis 22:11, 12).

As the voice from heaven faded, Abraham heard the bleating of a lamb. He turned and saw a lamb caught in a thicket. He took the lamb and put it on the altar in place of his son, Isaac. God had provided the sacrifice. Abraham praised JEHOVAH JIREH, God, my Provider.

This was a prophetic moment in history when God, our Provider, prepared us for the coming of His Son to this earth as ". . . the Lamb of God, who takes away the sin of the world" (John 1:29).

JEHOVAH JIREH, God, is my Provider. Jesus became the curse on the cross, dying in our place to destroy the works of evil and the curse and consequences of sin. Jesus is our salvation. He is the supplier of every good and perfect gift that flows to us from God, the Father, through Him.

Whatever your need is today, look to Jesus, the messenger of God who brings God's provisions into your life. Whatever your need is, God is bigger than your need. Stop looking at lack and start looking to God. Stop looking at what you can't do and start looking at what, with God's power and help, you can do.

Many years ago, when I was a student in college, I learned what my blessing-pact covenant with God meant. I was going to school full-time and was married. I made $35 a week working as a custodian. Every Sunday I put $3.50 in the collection plate as my tithe. That was my covenant with God; the tithe belonged to Him. It was my joy to bring it into the storehouse.

I'll never forget one harsh winter day in Kankakee, Illinois, where I lived on the edge of the Olivet College campus. I didn't have any money. There wasn't any food left in the house. I had a big need.

I began the day by reading and claiming this promise in Philippians 4:19 (KJV): ". . . my God shall supply all your need according to his riches in glory by Christ Jesus." I said, "Father, You are my supplier. You're my Provider. I don't know how You are going to meet my need, but I have been faithful in tithing and I know that somehow You are going to take care of me."

When I went to the mailbox that morning, I found an envelope. I don't know how it got there, I don't know where it came from. Nothing was written on the envelope. When I opened it, ten dollars in cash fell out.

Many times since I have again learned that God is my Provider, JEHOVAH JIREH.

> God has infinite ways of supplying your needs.

God Becomes Your Protector

The second benefit of the blessing-pact covenant with God is that you will live under His protection. Not to tithe is like driving our car down the road with the oil light on and doing nothing about it. If you ignore the oil light, you will eventually destroy the engine and pay the price.

Do you know that if you do not give the first tenth of your tithe to God, the devil will get it? You will not keep it for yourself. You may fool yourself into thinking you are going to keep it, but you won't. Someway, somehow, the devil will take it. Malachi 3:8–11 teaches us that not to give God the tithe is to rob Him and live under a curse. People who choose not to tithe ignore the warning light. They may get by for a while, but sooner or later they are going to reap financial losses.

In Malachi 3:11 we are promised that if we will bring the tithe into the storehouse, "I will prevent pests from devouring your crops, and the vines in your field will not cast their fruit. . . ."

You Become a Participant With God

The third benefit of a blessing-pact with God and tithing is that you stop being a spectator and become a participant. As you participate in tithing, you become a partner in the work of God on this earth.

You will never feel part of your church until you become a participant by giving of your money and time. No matter how good the sermons, the music, and the fellowship, your church will not come fully alive for you and impact your life until you pay the price. When you withhold your tithes, not only do you rob God and hurt yourself, but you diminish your church.

Those who give nothing, get nothing.
Those who give something, get something.
Those who give much, get much.

You Qualify for God's Promise

The fourth advantage of your blessing-pact covenant with God is that all the promises of financial prosperity become your inheritance. Here are three promises from the Word of God:

- "Honor the Lord by giving him the first part of all your income, and he will fill your barns with wheat and barley and overflow your wine vats with the finest wines" (Proverbs 3:9, 10 TLB).
- "Bring the whole tithe into the storehouse, that there may be food in my house. Test me in this," says the Lord Almighty, "and see if I will not throw open the floodgates of heaven and pour out so much blessing that you will not have room enough for it" (Malachi 3:10).
- "For if you give, you will get! Your gift will return to you in full and overflowing measure, pressed down, shaken together to make room for more, and running over . . ." (Luke 6:38 TLB).

These promises are yours if you will make a blessing-pact covenant with God and will faithfully keep your end of the agreement.

You Learn That Tithing Pays

It pays rich dividends to have a blessing-pact with God and pay your tithe. Perhaps you are suffering financial anxiety; there is never enough money to go around. After years of pastoral experience and study in the Word of God, I am convinced that your first step to getting on top of your finances is to start by giving 10 percent to God. I don't believe you can be successful in managing your finances until you start tithing. Tithing is the first step to financial success.

Let me ask you a question. How can God trust you with more until you can manage what He has been giving you? The first step in correct money management is to give God the first tenth off the top.

A friend of mine told me this about her tithing.

Because I tithe, God blesses my life in the following ways. When I was separated and struggling to make ends meet as a single working parent, I began to tithe after I recommitted to Jesus Christ. Within one month I received a raise equivalent to my tithe. The second month, the person buying some property I owned began doubling her payments. When I needed a lump sum of money, she paid off the contract early with a balloon payment. But I think the best part of tithing is the personal sense of well-being that comes from knowing I did the right thing with my money, and God never lets me down. If you will take that step of faith, He will not let you down, either. He is faithful.

Recently I received a phone call that a dear friend of mine had died. She was a charter member of the church I started when I left seminary in 1963, one of the sweetest, dearest, most Christlike people I ever knew. When I met her in 1963, she must have been in her sixties. She lived in a little house on the edge of town. She was a widow who took in ironing and cared for little children. Though she didn't have much of this world's goods, she was the most generous, giving person I have ever known.

This lady tithed her time to God by being volunteer custodian in our church. I was amazed to discover that this woman gave more money to the church than anyone else in the congregation.

When I heard that she had gone to be with Jesus, I remembered His command to lay up treasures in heaven and the realization came to me that she had gone to be where her treasures and heart were. I could almost hear Jesus saying to her, "Well done, thou good and faithful servant. Enter into the joy of thy Lord" (*see* Matthew 25:21).

The time to make your blessing-pact covenant with God is *now*.

THIRTEEN

The Harvest Principle

Today's seeds are tomorrow's harvest.

I want you to think about your brain. If it's average size, it weighs somewhere between eight and ten pounds. What it does is incredible. Your brain:

- stores information
- receives and sends out messages
- controls and directs the functions of your body
- solves problems
- imagines that which is not and brings it into existence
- makes judgments
- thinks and reasons
- monitors all your emotions

Studies of our brain have revealed that there is difference between the right side of our brain and the left side. The left side of our brain is the logical, thinking part, while the right side is intuitive and creative.

In the Western world, we have spent a lot of time developing the left side of our brain but have not spent as much time developing the right side. The right side of our brain is where the spiritual dimension is. That's where God has planted the gift of faith within you. That's where you have the ability to cooperate with God and visualize, dream, and create, to bring into existence that which is not yet here.

In Romans 10:17 (KJV) we read, "So then faith cometh by hearing, and hearing by the word of God." When you get into the Word of God and ask the Holy Spirit to illuminate the Word and make it come alive within you, it does. The deepest level of life that brings health and well-being to all areas of your life is the spiritual. In this chapter I want to speak to you in the fourth dimension, in the language of the Spirit. I want to communicate to you heart-to-heart, on the spiritual level.

Perhaps you are all bogged down because all you see is the physical. You think you have money problems when your real problem is spiritual. Let me ask you a question. Right now in your life, are you seeing lack or are you seeing the abundance that God wants to bring into your life? Are you thinking about what you don't have, or are you seeing that God wants to pour prosperity into your life?

There is something a whole lot more tragic than economic poverty. Do you know what it is? It is poverty of the mind and of the spirit. Jesus has come to give us life and to give us life more abundantly (*see* John 10:10).

Let me share with you a fantastic miracle story recorded in 1 Kings 17. Now I need to caution you that this story can only truly be understood by using the right side of your brain. The real understanding of the story is in the fourth dimension, through eyes of faith.

This true story is about a widow who lived in the village of Zarephath with her young son. There was a famine throughout the land, and this mother and her son were down to their last meal. As this widow cried out to God, He sent her a messenger and gave her an opportunity to have her needs met.

Some of you have tremendous needs right now. Financial anxiety has created knots in the pit of your stomach. You face unpaid bills. You feel like you're underneath the financial pile instead of on top. God, your heavenly Father, knows this, and He wants to generously supply all your needs according to His riches in glory in Christ Jesus (*see* Philippians 4:19).

The messenger of God to this poor widow was the prophet Elijah. It happened that Elijah didn't have anything to eat, either. Here was God's man, a prophet, and he, too, found himself in deep economic need. But God, his Provider, had promised to provide for his needs. Out in the wilderness, God had fed Elijah by having the ravens bring him bread and meat each morning and evening. There the prophet drank from the brook. But after a while, due to the lack of rainfall, the brook dried up. It was at this point that God told Elijah to go to the village of Zarephath, where a widow would feed him.

When Elijah arrived, the widow was outside gathering sticks for a fire. When the prophet asked her for something to eat, she said, "I swear by the Lord your God that I haven't a single piece of bread in the house. And I have only a handful of flour left and a little cooking oil in the bottom of the jar. I was just gathering a few sticks to cook this last meal, and then my son and I must die of starvation" (1 Kings 17:12 TLB). You talk about being in need!

So what did the prophet do? "Elijah said to her, 'Don't be afraid! Go ahead and cook that "last meal," but bake me a little loaf of bread first; and afterwards there will still be enough food for you and your son. For the Lord God of Israel says that there will always be plenty of flour and oil left in your containers until the time when the Lord sends rain, and the crops grow again!' " (1 Kings 17:13, 14 TLB).

The nerve of this man! Here is a widow woman down to her last meal. She has no food in the house, no money to buy more, and no place to get it, anyway. And what does the prophet do? Does he sympathize with her? Not really. He asks her, of all things, to give him a meal first.

Why? Because she needed to get her mind off starvation and poverty and believe that God would supply. She had to plant a seed at the point of her need. She had to take a positive action that would release her faith to believe in the God of the impossible.

> To really change your economic need,
> you've got to change your thinking.

Your most important need is to see God, who is a bountiful supplier. You must give at the point of your need, releasing your faith and giving God a seed that He can use to bring the harvest in your life.

What would you do if you were the widow? She received the Word of the Lord. She put her faith into action and it became her seed of faith. She took what she had—all that she had— baked the bread, and gave it in faith to the prophet Elijah.

The result was a miracle. "So she did as Elijah said, and she and Elijah and her son continued to eat from her supply of flour and oil as long as it was needed. For no matter how much they used, there was always plenty left in the containers, just as the Lord had promised through Elijah!" (1 Kings 17:15, 16 TLB).

> At the end of every rainbow is God.

Five Laws of the Harvest

Seed time and harvest   Before moving to Portland in 1969, I pastored a church in the middle of wheat country in Lawrence, Kansas.

Lawrence was surrounded by huge farms. I can remember driving down the country roads on the way to visit parishioners. It was an awesome sight to look out across those golden wheat fields standing on the verge of another bumper harvest. How did such a beautiful harvest of grain come about? One thing is for sure: It didn't just happen. Months before, the farmers went out and toiled in their fields to prepare the soil and then, with expectation of the harvest, they planted the seeds. You see, written into the very core of nature is a principle that the farmers understood: Today's seeds are tomorrow's harvest

In Genesis 8:22 we read that the Lord declared, "As long as the earth endures, seedtime and harvest . . . will never cease."

Sowing and reaping   The Apostle Paul teaches the eternal law of sowing and reaping as follows: "Do not be deceived: God cannot be mocked. A man reaps what he sows" (Galatians 6:7). This is a universal, eternal law of God. God cannot be mocked. Whatever a man says or does, this law does not change. Your choice is whether to plant good seeds or bad seeds. Every day of your life, you are planting either good seeds or bad seeds. In your economic life you are planting good seeds or bad seeds. There are no shortcuts to success. To reap a bountiful harvest, you must sow good seeds.

Everything worthwhile starts with a tiny seed. As you drive through the great apple orchards of the Northwest, you see the trees filled with delicious apples and your taste buds begin to water. It's another miracle of the harvest right before your very eyes.

Did you ever stop to think that every apple tree started with a tiny seed? And each seed has the explosive possibility of producing a healthy, strong tree filled each year with many bushels of apples. Think how many hundreds of thousands of times its own weight one little seed produces in the miracle of the harvest.

One of the most powerful economic spiritual laws that you need to understand is this one of sowing and reaping. The seeds you sow now set in motion the harvest you will live with tomorrow.

In the early days of New Hope Community Church, God brought into our fellowship a dear senior citizen named Jenny Spencer. God used this woman to teach me a very important lesson about how giving is a seed that we sow.

Jenny was up in years and was not able to attend many services, but she did catch the spirit and vision of New Hope, and she loved her church. One day as I was visiting with her in her mobile home, right in the middle of our visit she smiled at me and said, "I am so glad you're here, Dale, because I needed to give my seed-faith to help purchase that new land for our church."

When she handed me the large gift, I thought I shouldn't receive it, because it was too much for her to give. I didn't really know her financial situation, but I imagined that she needed to watch her pennies. I acted hesitant when she handed me the check, so she said, "Take it! I want to give it." Then she said, "I need to give."

We prayed together, and it seemed Jesus was very close to us that day.

As I stepped out on the porch and said good-bye to Jenny, I'll never forget what she said with tears in her eyes. "I am so glad you came today. I haven't been able to get to church, and I needed to give my seed-faith offering to the Lord."

The lesson I learned from Jenny was that regardless of whether we are young or elderly, have little of this world's goods or much, we all have the same need. We need to give.

It's not by accident that Jesus said, "Give first and you will receive" (*see* Luke 6:38). I've discovered that when people give and when I give, these wonderful things happen:

- I'm set free from selfishness.
- I break out of a negative cycle.
- I put my trust in God, my Provider.
- I become a partner with God in His work and miracles.
- I am filled with the joy of the Lord.
- Generosity flows through my spirit.

The giving of our tithes and offerings to the Lord is one of the ways we keep planting good seeds. Someone said to me, "Pastor, I've been tithing for two weeks and I haven't seen anything good happen." Your job is to sow good seed. Keep giving. Keep sowing. If you keep sowing good seeds, you are going to reap a good harvest. But it does take time for all seeds to grow.

Lord of the harvest Where does the seed come from that is placed in your care? James tells us, "Every good and perfect gift cometh from above" (*see* James 1:17). God is a generous and bountiful giver.

- God owns all the real estate. "The earth is the Lord's, and the fulness thereof; the world, and they that dwell therein" (Psalms 24:1 KJV).
- God owns all the cattle. "For every animal of the forest is mine, and the cattle on a thousand hills" (Psalms 50:10).
- God owns the financial world. "The silver is mine, and the gold is mine, saith the Lord of hosts" (Haggai 2:8 KJV).

God, who has it all, who created it all, who owns it all, gives you material blessings. He shares with you. He entrusts to you what is His. You are to be a steward of what God has given to you. Are you being a faithful steward or an unfaithful steward? Before God can trust you with more, you must do a good job with what you've been given. If you can't manage a little and be faithful to God, you sure won't be able to manage a lot and be faithful to God.

Before you can be successful in financial management, you've got to get it settled who is the Lord. Consider 2 Corinthians 9:10, 11: "Now he who supplies seed to the sower and bread for food will also supply and increase your store of seed and will enlarge the harvest of your righteousness. You will be made rich in every way so that you can be generous on every occasion. . . ." This is all conditioned upon your knowing who the Lord of the harvest is and making God your source.

What about the timing of the harvest? One of our problems is that we are of the "now" generation. You don't plant beans and go out the next day and expect to pick them.

> God is in charge of the timing of the harvest.
> Our job is to sow the seed.

Proportionate return   How does a farmer get the best crop? I have never been a farmer, but from what farmers tell me, if you want to have the very best corn crop the following year, you save back the finest, best ears for planting. In other words, you plant the best and you harvest the best.

Consider Proverbs 3:9, 10 (TLB): "Honor the Lord by giving him the first part of all your income, and he will fill your barns with wheat and barley and overflow your wine vats with the finest wines." In other words, give to God off the top, give Him the first, give Him the best, and He in turn will give you the best. What you receive back will be based on what you give.

You can't give God the money that is "left over" and expect an abundant return. Most people have nothing left over to give. You want God's best? Then give Him your best. Give Him the first tenth off the top of your income. Give Him some of your best time off the top.

There is a law of proportionate return. "Remember this: Whoever sows sparingly will also reap sparingly, and whosoever sows generously will also reap generously" (2 Corinthians 9:6).

Multiplication I only have to look at the ministry of New Hope Community Church to see that God multiplies the seeds we plant. In the summer of 1972, Margi and I had an enormous need. The call of God was on our lives for pastoral ministry, but we didn't have a church to pastor. The truth is, nobody wanted us. The only thing we had was some equity in what we called our "honeymoon house" in Portland. It was our hideaway from the world, something very special in our lives. We both have great memories of that first house.

We willingly and in faith sold that house, took the equity, and planted it as a seed to launch New Hope Community Church. It was everything we had. That first seed was used of God to bring fruit. And with fruit came more seeds. People came, and in faith gave their tithes and offerings. They gave of themselves in ministry, and the Lord of the harvest multiplied and blessed.

Please remember two things: From whom much is given, much will be required; the seeds you sow today will become the harvest you reap tomorrow.

FOURTEEN

The Thanksgiving Principle

"In every thing give thanks: for this is the will of God in Christ Jesus concerning you" (1 Thessalonians 5:18 KJV).

Have you ever felt that you were at the end of your rope, just barely holding on with your teeth? How do you get up when everything is going wrong?

The way to keep going and to be victorious is to practice the thanksgiving principle. In fact, if you will practice this one principle, nothing can defeat you for long. With this thanksgiving principle your spirit will rise to the top again and again.

In the real world, it's often hard to keep a positive attitude. That's why I firmly believe in the value of our national holiday of Thanksgiving. Traditionally on that day we gorge ourselves with marvelous foods, but Thanksgiving is much more than that. It is a day to remember God and be thankful. The Bible tells us, "When you have eaten and are satisfied, praise the Lord your God for the good land he has given you. Be careful that you do not forget the Lord your God . . ." (Deuteronomy 8:10, 11).

Our Pilgrim fathers were not rich or powerful. They were not highly educated. They were simple, common folk. It took them 120 days to cross the Atlantic in their little ship of 90 tons. History records that they crossed the ocean during one of the wildest winters ever to sweep the North Atlantic.

The *Mayflower* landed in New England in December, in the cold of winter. Years earlier, Columbus had landed farther south in October and his crew had mutinied. They were summer sailors. But no one among the Pilgrims wanted to mutiny. During that first harsh New England winter, ninety were sick at one time and only seven were well enough to move around and care for the others. One by one they died—wives, husbands, children—and they laid them in the frozen earth. Fifty-one out of 102 died that first year. Yet on that first Thanksgiving Day, they found so much to be thankful for. Yes, Thanksgiving is much more than just another holiday; it is a spirit that lifts our spirit to His Spirit.

In the Scriptures we are exhorted with these words, "Enter into his gates with thanksgiving, and into his courts with praise: be thankful unto him, and bless his name" (Psalms 100:4 KJV).

Gaining Altitude With the Attitude of Gratitude

Choose, cultivate, and express the attitude of gratitude in your daily life and you are going to be a happy person.

What a difference there is between the attitude of gratitude and the bad attitude of ingratitude. We see the contrast between the two in an encounter Jesus had with ten outcast lepers. Leprosy was a dreaded disease that ate away the human body. If you had leprosy, you had to leave normal people and go and live among the lepers.

When these ten lepers saw Jesus, they cried out, "Have mercy on us." Jesus, moved with compassion, healed them, and they were made clean and whole.

Watch what happened. "One of them, when he saw he was healed, came back, praising God in a loud voice. He threw himself at Jesus' feet and thanked him—and he was a Samaritan" (Luke 17:15, 16). This man, who had been the victim of the most horrible disease anyone could have, was from a mongrel race. He had lived in the pit of emotional despair. Now he ceased to feel sorry for himself and gained altitude with the attitude of gratitude!

Ingratitude is a very serious sin. First of all, it grieves the spirit of the giver. "Jesus asked, 'Were not all ten cleansed? Where are the other nine? Was no one found to return and give praise to God except this foreigner?' " (Luke 17:17, 18). The ingratitude of these thankless nine grieved the spirit of our Lord Jesus.

Ingratitude also dwarfs us on the inside. It is a very serious sin that leads to worse sins. In Romans 1, we read a vivid description of people who were living like animals, engaging in all kinds of sexual perversion. So wicked and corrupt was their behavior that the Scripture says God gave them up to their own self-destruction. But when you read this passage of Scripture, you'll notice that their downward slide all started with the sin of ingratitude. "For although they knew God, they neither glorified him as God nor gave thanks to him, but their thinking became futile and their foolish hearts were darkened" (Romans 1:21).

I'm writing to someone who needs to get up right now and get out of the pit of self-pity. Let Jesus touch you with His power and strength. Rise up and gain altitude with the attitude of gratitude.

> Nothing breeds discontent within
> a person like ingratitude.

Show me a person who is griping and picking, and I'll show you a person who is ungrateful for what she's been given. How do you change from being an ungrateful person to having an attitude of gratitude that makes you and everyone else around you happy? You do it by confessing your sin of ingratitude and asking Jesus to forgive and change you. Then by choice you start practicing the principle of thanksgiving.

Refill Your Think Tank With Thanks

No one enjoys having his finger smashed by a hammer. When you lose your job, it's unreal to say, "Praise the Lord, I lost my job." A whole lot of bad things happen to you and me, and there is no way we're happy about them. We'd rather not have them happen.

Yet we are told to give thanks for *everything*. That means we are not to surrender the leadership of our lives to circumstances. Whatever happens, good or bad, we are to keep on practicing the principle of thanksgiving because God is in charge. God is at work to bring good out of bad. Say, "Thank You, Jesus, that even though I don't understand what's happening to me right now, I can praise Your name that You're going to bring me through this victorious."

As you live day by day you cannot afford to let the world squeeze you into its negative mold. If you do, you're going to walk around like a sad sack. You're going to be blinded to the blessings. You're going to center on all the wrong things. You're going to blow up little things and make mountains out of molehills. You're going to lose your perspective.

Day by day we need to come back to the teachings of God's Word and renew our minds. How do you renew your mind? You do it by taking the Word of God and obeying it. In everything that happens in your life, keep on thanking and praising God. In Ephesians 5:20 (KJV) we read, "Giving thanks always for all things unto God. . . ." That means that you just keep giving thanks, and as you give thanks, you will refill your think tank with clear thinking.

Think about all you have been given by God, "Who has blessed us with every blessing in heaven because we belong to Christ" (Ephesians 1:3 TLB).

- Thank Him because you belong to God's family.
- Thank Him for your uniqueness as His child.
- Thank Him for your age and its blessings.
- Thank Him for your family, friendships, and relationships with other people.
- Thank Him for the gift of life and the opportunity to serve Christ and glorify Him through your life.

The practice of giving thanks in everything is a sure cure for emotional depression.

A fine young man came to me for some counseling. He had been to one therapist after another seeking a solution to his depression. He had carefully analyzed and scrutinized his emotional life with a variety of professionals, but had found no relief from his everyday doom and gloom.

I asked my young friend if he was ready to take the cure. At this point he was willing to try just about anything. I opened the Bible and turned to the thanksgiving principle I have shared with you. I challenged my friend to put this principle into practice many times throughout the day: In everything give thanks.

Although he didn't feel like doing it, he did it because he had made a commitment to this principle. To help him put the principle into practice, I asked him to make a list of twenty-five things for which he was thankful. At first he said this was impossible. However, I helped him get started on his list and before he left, he had twenty-five things written down. I told him to read the list every morning and throughout the day.

When the young man came back to see me in a week, he was a changed man. The doom and the gloom were gone. He had a smile on his face and a glow in his eyes. He was a brand-new, happy person. He had an optimism and enthusiasm about life that he hadn't known in years. The thanksgiving principle that worked wonders for him will do the same for you.

Praise Is a Matter of Life and Breath

> "Let everything that has breath
> praise the Lord . . ." (Psalms 150:6).

Praise is one step higher up the ladder than giving thanks. Praise is a very important ingredient in spiritual life. God the Father delights in hearing us praise Him. Scripture commands us to praise God. Also, praise is a measure of our spiritual vitality, a tonic that keeps our spiritual lives fresh and filled with enthusiasm.

Several years ago, when I appeared on the "700 Club," I met Ben, the shows's cohost. As he was driving me back to the airport to catch my plane, we were sharing about how important praise is in the life of the Christian. Ben shared with me a spiritual insight into this familiar verse, "Enter his gates with thanksgiving and his courts with praise . . ." (Psalms 100:4). Ben pointed out that we come to the Lord through expressing our thanksgiving, and that's wonderful. But we enter into His inner courts, into His very presence, by the expression of words of praise from our hearts. Praise is more than just saying thank-you; it is admiration and worship. You might say that it's letting out all the stops.

Praise God for who He is. "How great Thou art!" Praise him for being a God of mercy and love, a holy God, a steadfast and dependable God, the God of order and perfect plans. Praise God for what He does. He takes care of His own. He gives us all His love. He supplies all our needs according to His riches. He is with us in good times and difficult times. In Him we have our life, our being, and our assurance of final victory.

The greatest way that you and I can show our thanks to God is to praise Him.

PART FOUR

*Be Successful
in Fulfilling
Your Destiny*

FIFTEEN

The Joy Principle

"... The joy of the Lord is your strength"
(Nehemiah 8:10 KJV).

As long as I live, I will never forget our first Christmas together after Margi and I were married. Our little honeymoon house was all decorated and lit with Christmas lights. I had so much fun shopping for Margi and picking out just the right gifts of love. I purchased some colorful wrapping paper and wrapped each of the gifts myself. I could hardly wait to give her these surprises. In fact, I couldn't wait; I gave her the gifts early.

All excited and with tremendous joy, I brought out my gifts and gave them to Margi. I was totally unprepared for what happened next. Instead of being happy, she was sad. Instead of being filled with joy, she almost cried.

What robbed her of her joy? Instead of focusing on the gift, she was seeing the poor, amateur job of gift wrapping. I learned that how a gift is wrapped makes a difference to this woman. Since that day I have always gotten someone else to help me wrap Margi's gifts so they would have that touch of beauty and finesse that she likes.

In a little while she started laughing and realized how silly it was to let the wrapping ruin her joy. Then she really enjoyed the gifts of love I had given to her.

That day we learned a very important lesson together: The true joy of Christmas is not whether you have the right wrappings. It's not even whether you have the right gift. The joy that Jesus came to give is an inside job.

How do you get the most out of life? How do you enjoy your blessings to the hilt? How do you overcome trouble? The answers to these very important questions are to be found in the joy principle: ". . . The joy of the Lord is your strength" (Nehemiah 8:10 KJV).

Jesus' Joy

In the Bible Jesus is described as ". . . full of joy through the Holy Spirit . . ." (Luke 10:21). He was joy, is joy, and always will be joy. This cannot be said about any other religious leader. You will not even find the word *joy* in a psychology book, because joy is a Christian emotion. Joy is something that is brought into our lives and world through Jesus.

It was His joy that sustained Jesus at the cross. Here's what the Bible says: "Let us fix our eyes on Jesus, the author and perfecter of our faith, who for the joy set before him endured the cross, scorning its shame, and sat down at the right hand of the throne of God" (Hebrews 12:2).

One reason the Holy Scripture was written was that you might have joy. In the receiving of God's Word is the gift of joy. Jesus said, ". . . I have come that they may have life, and have it to the full" (John 10:10). A part of this full life is to have joy, wonderful joy, on the inside.

Jesus intends to put His own joy inside of you. When you receive Jesus as your Lord and Savior, you receive your birthright and inheritance of joy. Listen to what Jesus said in John 15:11 (KJV): "These things have I spoken unto you, that my joy might remain in you, and that your joy might be full."

Jesus spoke these words for you, to you. In giving us joy, Jesus gives us Himself.

Notice the words, "remain in you." This reminds us that joy can come and go. But it is Jesus' purpose and will that His joy remain in us. A lot of times when it is supposed to remain, we let it go.

To have the joy of the Lord as we should, we've got to learn how to have it remain. For our joy to remain, we have to remain in His presence. There is no other place to get joy except in the presence of the Lord. People look for it everywhere, but joy is ours by abiding in Jesus.

The psalmist knew where you could find joy when he said, "You have made known to me the path of life; you will fill me with joy in your presence, with eternal pleasures at your right hand" (Psalms 16:11).

As a child of God it is your birthright, it is your privilege, to remain in the presence of Jesus so his joy will be within you. Joy is one of the fruits of the Spirit that is ours through abiding in Christ.

As we fellowship with Jesus,
the joy of the Lord becomes our strength.

The Thief Is Out to Rob You of Your Joy

John 10:10 (KJV) tells us, "The thief cometh not, but for to steal, and to kill, and to destroy. . . ." Who wants to rob you and steal your joy? The same one who is out to destroy you: the devil. The devil doesn't come to encourage you; he comes to discourage you. He doesn't bring you good gifts; he comes to rob you and take the good gifts from you that God has given. You need to know who the devil is, and you need to know that he is out to rob you of your joy.

Why does the devil want to rob you of your joy? Because he wants to rob you of your strength. The joy of the Lord is your strength. When the devil robs you of your joy, he can do with you just about as he pleases, because you don't have any resistance or power. You've lost your joy.

> **Don't let the devil get your joy.**

You go to church and get all charged with joy, but what happens after you leave? On the way home, you and your wife get into a discussion over what the preacher said. You say he said this and she says he didn't say that at all. You try to prove that you're right and she's wrong. She tries to prove that she's right and you're wrong. What happened to the joy of the Lord you had? You've just let the devil rob you of your joy.

Jesus wants you to have joy all the time, not just on Sunday morning in church or not just when everything is going right. When little things happen that irritate you, He still wants you to have joy. Joy comes from the inside out.

A couple of years ago I performed one of the most beautiful wedding celebrations I have ever seen. The bride's gown was uniquely beautiful. The bridesmaids looked like they had stepped out of a fashion magazine. Everything was the finest. The father and mother of the bride had put out big bucks to make this the wedding of all weddings.

In the midst of the ceremony, I looked down at the bride's

mother and saw she had a big frown on her face. She looked like she was about ready to kill somebody. Here was this great celebration that she had looked forward to and planned for years—the wedding of her only daughter—and she wasn't enjoying it at all.

Afterwards I found out what had robbed the mother of her joy. The florist had put the wrong color roses in the mother's corsage, so she sat there in a miserable state of mind and missed the joy of her only daughter's wedding.

Let the joy of the Lord be your strength, and don't let the devil get your joy.

Overcome Trouble With Turned-on Joy

How well do you handle trouble? When trouble comes, do you throw up your hands in despair? Do you give up the joy of the Lord? If you give up your joy, you become weak at the knees. If you surrender your joy, you become defenseless. What you've got to learn to do, no matter what happens, is never give up your joy.

> "Rejoice in the Lord alway:
> and again I say, Rejoice"
> (Philippians 4:4 KJV).

In Habakkuk 3:17 we read about a man who is having a lot of trouble. Everything is going wrong. His fig trees won't bud, there are no grapes on the vine, his olive crop fails, the fields produce no food, there are no sheep in his pen, no cattle in the stalls. He's in a bad way.

I want you to see how he got on top of his troubles. He says one important word: *yet.* "Yet I will rejoice in the Lord, I will be joyful in God my Savior" (Habakkuk 3:18).

Here is the road to victory. Never let the devil steal your joy. He may take other things from you, but he can't take your joy if you don't let him.

In the Old Testament, the children of Israel were often outnumbered in battle. They would call a solemn fast and cry out to God. God never said to them, "Give Me more swordsmen. Give Me more chariots." Instead He said, "Give Me the singers, the trumpet blowers, the musicians, the choir. Put them at the front and let them lead praises to God." When Israel begain praising God, He always turned the tide and brought them victory.

Joy is not something just for the morning. It's not something you have only when everything is going well. Joy is something to have in good times and in bad times. Joy is yours in Jesus. Joy is what we are to practice in season and out of season.

> **In times of trouble, say,**
> **"The joy of the Lord is my strength."**

Don't sit around feeling sorry for yourself in time of trouble. Don't sit around shrinking in fear. In times of trouble you are to offer up a sacrifice with shouts of joy to the Lord. There are times where it is easy to thank God and to sing and shout hallelujah to the Lord. In times of trouble, it is not so easy; it becomes a sacrifice. A sacrifice is something that is costly. Sometimes you have to make yourself offer it. Learning to offer up the sacrifice with shouts of joy in times of trouble is the key that unlocks the door to victory.

Pay-Back Time Is Coming

Remember Job? The devil attacked him and took his family, his house, his possessions—everything he had. Robbed of his joy, Job was left desolate and despondent, wanting to die.

When Job finally made up his mind that the joy of the Lord was his strength, that he wasn't going to let the devil rob him of the joy he had in his relationship with God, he began to praise and exalt God. God came to his rescue and not only gave him back everything he had lost, but gave it back multiplied. God blessed Job with abundance.

> Joy not only pays off; joy pays back.

In Jeremiah we read that the land had become desolate. The streets of Jerusalem were deserted; the people were beaten. But Jeremiah, speaking the words of the Lord, told them that if they would sound the voice of joy, if they would bring a thanksgiving offering to the house of God, God would restore the land. God is the great Restorer. If you will not let the devil rob you of your joy, the Word of God promises that God will restore to you anything and everything the devil has taken and give you more than you had before. With the joy of the Lord in your heart and on your lips, there is no way the devil can keep your goods. For God is on your side, and He's going to bring it back to you, multiplied many times over.

"Rejoice in the Lord alway: and again I say, Rejoice" (Philippians 4:4 KJV).

SIXTEEN

The Right-Choice Principle

Responder or reactor: The choice is yours.

Success in life is determined by the choices we make. God has given each of us the awesome freedom of making choices. As Mary Crowley says, "We are free up to the point of choice, then the choice controls the chooser." Or as Stanley Baldwin puts it, "We make our choices and then our choices make us."

Identical twin sisters grew up with an alcoholic father. When they reached adulthood, one twin became an alcoholic, the other an abstainer. The sisters were interviewed by a psychologist who asked the first twin why she became an alcoholic. She responded, "Well, what do you expect from a daughter of an alcoholic?" In a separate session the psychologist asked the second twin why she had become an abstainer. She said, "Well, what do you expect from a daughter of an alcoholic?"

What happens to us in everyday life is not nearly as important as how we choose to respond. In order for you to make the right choices, you need to understand the difference between reacting and responding.

Description of a reactor The battle is on. A reactor takes his anger out on others. He has to prove who's right and who's wrong. In reacting, he loses his freedom to choose and does the opposite of what he should do. The reactor is defensive, creates tension, blames others. He gives off vibrations that say, "Stay away from me." He ends up getting ulcers.

Description of a responder A responder keeps his cool despite pressure. He listens to the other person, tries to see things from the other's viewpoint. He gives warmth and understanding, communicates clearly, says no with a smile, makes the other person feel good even when he disagrees with him. The responder gives off an aura of love. He stays at ease and does not get all tensed up.

Jesus Was Always a Responder

Jesus came to teach us and model for us a better way to live and relate. No one has ever suffered more from the consequences of other people's misdeeds than Jesus. Jesus, who never showed anything but love to other people, was treated more unjustly and unfairly than anyone who has ever lived.

Look at Jesus being crucified on the cross. Hear Him say, "Father, forgive them for they know not what they do." Jesus died on the cross, giving us a new and better way to live and relate. Jesus invites you to come and be His follower, to become a citizen of the Kingdom of God, to learn how to live by Kingdom principles.

Listen to some of the Kingdom principles that teach us not to be a reactor but a responder:

"The law of Moses says, 'If a man gouges out another's eye, he must pay with his own eye. If a tooth gets knocked out, knock out the tooth of the one who did it.' But I say: Don't resist violence! If you are slapped on one cheek, turn the other too."

Matthew 5:38, 39 TLB

Turning the other cheek is an advance step in Kingdom living. It means that no matter how badly another person treats you or acts, you do not react with the same abuse but through the power of Christ within you, you choose to live and relate in a better way.

Reacting is always the destructive way. It never solves anything. It destroys relationships. By contrast, responding always opens the door for renewed friendship, breaks down the barriers, creates good relationships, and produces healthy, happy people. Jesus calls us and empowers us to follow in His steps and become positive responders instead of negative reactors.

Respond for a Better Day

If you want to ruin a perfectly good day, just start reacting. On the other hand, if you want to have a beautiful day, follow Jesus' steps and become a responder. Every day is a new day. This is *your* day to become a positive responder.

Accept the fact that there are some things you cannot change. You cannot change another person. You cannot change what has happened. You have this day, this new day, to make the right choices.

As a manager, when your employer acts in a rude, thoughtless, inconsiderate manner, you choose whether to play his game and become a negative reactor, or take charge and respond.

Often when people are being dogmatic or acting ugly, they don't do it to hurt us. It generally means they are hurting. Someone has said, "Every obnoxious act is a cry for help."

Why do normal, good-natured people often turn into animals when they get behind the steering wheel of a car? The other day I was driving down the freeway. I don't think I did anything wrong; I was just driving along. Pretty soon a guy comes flying around me, gets right in front of me, and gives me the finger. Here I am, a pastor, and here's this guy I don't even know giving me this vulgar sign.

The thought came into my mind, *Shall I give him the sign back? I better not do that; somebody might see me. Well, maybe I could step on the gas and just bump his bumper a little bit. If I do that, somebody is going to get hurt. Maybe I could run him off the road and scream at him. If I do that, there's going to be a fight.*

Fortunately for me, I made the right choice. I decided not to let a guy who's obviously out of control ruin my day. So I said, "Jesus, help me. Bless that wild man." About then he got caught behind a car. As I passed him in the left lane, I just gave him a nice big smile. As I smiled, I felt the muscles in my body relax. It's so much better to be responders instead of negative reactors.

> **Jesus calls us to a better way to live—
> the way of being a responder.**

One of the number-one keys for me in choosing to respond instead of reacting is to stop and listen. Listen to the Holy Spirit as He gives you guidance. Listen to what the other person is saying. Nine times out of ten when I react, it's because I talk when I should be listening. When you listen to other people you affirm them as being worthwhile and entitled to their viewpoint, even though you do not agree with them. You also help them to get it off their chests and cool down.

Have you ever had one of your kids come in and say, "I hate school! I'm not going back to school anymore!"

The urge is to react. "What do you mean? You're going to school no matter what!"

What we need to do is respond and find out what's going on. What's the kid upset about? One mom discovered that her boy was saying he didn't want to go back to school because he mispronounced a word and was embarrassed and hurt by the kids' laughing. A little listening and warm understanding and he was all healed up, ready to go back to school.

Responders believe that other people have value and worth. No matter how a person may be acting, he or she is a human being of value. Treat that person as you want to be treated, the way Jesus taught you.

Respect other people and they will
respect you.
Love other people and they will
love you.
Treat other people as they want to be treated
and they will treat you as you want to be treated.

What You Give Is What You Get

Jesus teaches us that when we do good, God the Father brings us positive rewards. Jesus said, "Love your enemies! Do good to them! Lend to them! And don't be concerned about the fact that they won't repay. Then your reward from heaven will be very great . . ." (Luke 6:35 TLB).

You are free to choose. You can be either a negative reactor or a positive responder, but the choice you make sets into motion the treatment you will receive. In my book *You Can Win With Love,* I share this anecdote:

Once there was a little boy who was strongly admonished and rebuked by his mother. Later, out in the woods behind their house, he yelled at her and said, "I hate you!" Then he heard a voice (his echo) coming back to him, a stranger out in the woods saying, "I hate you! I hate you! I hate you!" It scared the wits out of him. He ran as fast as he could back to his mother and said, "Mother, there's a mean man in the woods. He's out there yelling, and saying, 'I hate you! I hate you! I hate you!' "

The perceptive mother said, "Go back out in the woods and yell as loud as you can, 'I love you! I love you! I love you!' " So the little boy did as his mother admonished him. He went out in the woods and yelled, "I love you! I love you! I love you!" Back came the echo, "I love you! I love you! I love you!" We also get what we give.

The Choice Is Yours

In our society today, many people want to enjoy all the benefits of freedom without taking responsibility for the choices they make. People want to blame society, teachers, parents, anything and everything except taking responsibility for their own choices.

Life is a series of choices. How you choose to give life today will determine what your life is going to be like tomorrow. For example, you can choose today to go out and get drunk, but when you do, you've chosen to feel miserable tomorrow.

To love is also your choice. You cannot avoid conflict in this life. You cannot avoid negative happenings. Sometimes you're going to be treated unfairly. But the choice of whether you're going to react negatively or respond positively is always yours.

The good news is that you don't have to have ulcers, high blood pressure, and heart problems because of choosing to react. With Christ's help you can learn to be a responder.

You can watch a person go about his daily activities for years and not learn a great deal about him. However, you can watch that person under adverse circumstances for five minutes and see whether he's learned to respond or react. Under pressure, we show what's really on the inside.

Jesus came to change us and transform us from the inside out. He gives us strength and power to do what we can't do by ourselves. In the pressure times, He enables us to make the right choice and respond instead of react.

**Make the right choice
to be a responder now.**

SEVENTEEN
The Broken-to-Bless Principle

In love's service, only broken hearts will do.

Why would a person need to be broken? What gain could come from pain?

God needs compassionate, caring people in this world to give His love to those who need it. There's no doubt about it: Great sensitivity comes to us only when we personally walk through suffering. How beautifully God uses broken hearts, made whole by His love, to bless others.

Someone has said, in love's service, only broken hearts will do.

> To grow a rose
> you have to have thorns.

Trouble Can Be Good for You

I said to a man going through a lot of trouble, "Trouble can be good for you."

He looked at me as if I didn't know what I was talking about and said, "You've got to be kidding!"

I said to my friend, "When you look trouble right in the eye and refuse to let it defeat you, when you make up your mind that, with Christ's help, you are going to overcome it, it's amazing what inner strength you will discover and what growth will take place within you."

> Tough times are times to triumph.

Trouble never leaves you the way it found you. It changes you into either a bitter person or a better person. Which it does is up to you. Every hardship in your life brings a wonderful opportunity for growth and development.

When trouble comes into your life, let it make you depend more on the Lord. Trouble can be like a refining fire that takes away pride and arrogance and makes you a more lovable person. Trouble can be the experience that brings compassion and understanding to your personality. Trouble can be the test that makes you reach down deep inside and develop the strengths of character you wouldn't have otherwise.

> If your life is going to be useful and used by God,
> you are not going to escape trouble.

I think Joseph suffered unjustly more than all the other characters in the Old Testament. As a boy, Joseph had an easy life. He was the favorite son. He got the special coat of many colors, and he was pampered and spoiled by his father. Only trouble and adversity could have prepared Joseph to have the character and the will to be second-in-command in Egypt. In other words, Joseph needed trouble to toughen him and make something out of him.

Psalms 105:17–19 teaches us something interesting about Joseph. ". . . He sent a man before them—Joseph, sold as a slave. They bruised his feet with shackles, his neck was put in irons, till what he foretold came to pass. . . ." In an old English translation, the last part of verse 18 reads, "iron came into his soul." In other words, God used the trouble that came to Joseph to toughen him and put iron in his soul.

Meanwhile, back in Joseph's home country, his family was experiencing a famine. In an attempt to save the family, the father sent the brothers to Egypt to buy grain. So it was that Joseph, second in command only to Pharaoh, stood facing the brothers who had sold him into slavery. Their fate and their lives were literally in his hands. What did he do? What emotions did he feel? The Scriptures tell us that he was overcome with emotion, that he couldn't control himself. "And he wept so loudly that the Egyptians heard him and Pharaoh's household heard about it" (Genesis 45:2).

Joseph, the man God had prepared through trouble, had been fine-tuned with compassion. Generously and with great love, he forgave his brothers. He embraced them, gave them grain, and opened his heart and home to them. What a reconciliation. What a restoration. What a triumph over trouble!

One of my favorite passages in the Old Testament is found in Genesis 50:19, 20. Listen to what Joseph said to his brothers: "Don't be afraid . . . You intended to harm me, but God intended it for good to accomplish what is now being done, the saving of many lives."

> In love's service, only broken hearts will do.

Turn Your Pain Into Gain

What would we do without caring persons? Remember the Good Samaritan in the Bible, how he cared about the man attacked by robbers? The Good Samaritan had nothing to gain by helping the victim, but he helped anyway. Like Jesus, he was moved with compassion for the man and helped him.

The victim in the story of the Good Samaritan illustrates three different ways we relate to others in our lives. The robbers beat him up. The priest and the Levite passed him up. The Good Samaritan, moved by compassion, lifted him up and cared for him. In every relationship we can choose to beat people up, pass them up, or lift them up.

You're certainly not going to have an effective Christian witness if you go around beating up people verbally. The scary thing is that you can verbally abuse people without realizing it. Stop and listen to your voice. Listen to what you are really saying to other people. Is it negative? Does it put them down? Do they hear threats from you? Or do they feel drawn to you by your warmth and love? Sometimes we beat up the people closest to us by taking out our anger on them.

Without compassion we will ignore people. We will pass them up when they need our help. Why was the Good Samaritan compassionate? Why did he stop when others passed by? I think it was because he knew what it was to suffer, and out of his suffering had come compassion.

Look for an Opportunity for Service

The greatest door-to-door Bible salesman of all time stuttered. He made up his mind that he was going to turn his disadvantage into advantage. After making the presentation with a lot of stuttering, he would close with these words: "Do you want to b-b-b-buy the Bible now or do you w-w-want me to r-r-read it to you?"

Take your adversities and turn them into assets, then use them to the glory of God. How do you do that? By depending on the Lord. By cooperating with Him. By believing that God turns adversity into striking opportunities. Remember, every adversity hides a possibility for ministry and service. You didn't go through this for nothing. You went through it so you could learn and use it to an advantage.

With God's help, turn every adversity into an advantage.

Thank God

Jesus turned His brokenness into blessing. He was unjustly accused, rejected, a man of sorrows, acquainted with grief, turned against by His own, crucified, and put to death on the cross.

The Scriptures tell us, "But he was pierced for our trans-gressions, he was crushed for our iniquities; the punishment that brought us peace was upon him, and by his wounds we are healed" (Isaiah 53:5).

> Jesus was broken to bless us.
> By the power of God, His brokenness
> was turned into a blessing.

Let God and His power heal your brokenness and use it to bless others. God specializes in turning pain into gain. God specializes in taking lives that have been broken, putting them back together, making them stronger than ever, and using them in wonderful ways to minister to others.

EIGHTEEN
The Greatness Principle

". . . Whoever wants to become great among you must be your servant" (Matthew 20:26).

Children are forever daydreaming about the exciting jobs they'll have when they grow up. They have a real desire to be great. It's surprising to see how early these ambitions sometimes develop. By the time a boy is three, he may already picture himself as somebody big and important, like a baseball pitcher, a policeman, or a fireman. Little sister is already being a good mother to her dolls, nursing people, or leaping tall buildings like Wonder Woman.

Aren't kids great? Not only are they great, but they have the desire to really be somebody when they grow up. What they are expressing is the same desire we all have. We all have the desire to be great—to be a somebody—to make our lives count for something.

Jesus gave us the greatness principle.

The disciples were human beings just like us. They had the same dreams, ambitions, and frailties we do. On more than one occasion, they had a dispute over who among them was the greatest. They argued about which of them was going to sit at Jesus' right hand in his coming Kingdom. Sometimes these discussions turned into verbal fights that caused bad feelings among the disciples.

Once Mrs. Zebedee, the mother of James and John, got into this jockeying for position. Her ambition was for her two sons to be at the top. She was not unlike a lot of mothers who have big dreams and hopes for their sons and daughters. She wanted people to think highly of her boys who had left their nets and followed the Messiah. She came right out with it and asked the Master to let her boys sit right beside Him in the Kingdom, one on the right and one on the left.

Just in case you are wondering how the other ten felt about this, check out Matthew 20:24. ". . . They were indignant. . . ." Guess why? No way were they going to give up their top spots without a fight. They got downright ticked-off over the idea that James and John might get ahead of them.

Sounds familiar, doesn't it? People haven't changed a whole lot since then.

Jesus answered the mother with this penetrating comment: "You don't know what you are asking" (v. 22). That must have stung! She really thought she knew what she wanted. In this world there are peons and there are kings. She wanted her boys to be right up there at the top, kings over all the others. Jesus seized the opportunity to explain to her and the others that His Kingdom was different from the world's system. In the Kingdom of God, people do not go around lording it over one another; they treat one another with love and respect.

Jesus seized the opportunity to teach His disciples the prime principle for greatness. ". . . Whoever wants to be great among you must be your servant" (Matthew 20:26).

You do want to be great, don't you? You do want to make your life count for something worthwhile. Then put this greatness principle into practice by doing these three things:

Serve Others

The greatest person who has ever lived came to this earth teaching us how to serve others. Jesus not only taught the Word, but He showed us how in His actions, so His greatness could be caught. Jesus commented on His own actions of service to His disciples when He said, "Now that I, your Lord and Teacher, have washed your feet, you also should wash one another's feet" (John 13:14).

You, too, can be great,
if you will just do what Jesus did.

When you serve others, it demonstrates your love for Jesus. "Again Jesus said, 'Simon son of John, do you truly love me?' He answered, 'Yes, Lord, you know that I love you.' Jesus said, 'Take care of my sheep' " (John 21:16). In other words, "If you love Me, then serve others in My name. Do for them what I have done for you."

Serving others always leads to a great life. The happiest people I've ever known have been people who devoted their lives to serving others.

Earl Nightingale tells this story. On a stormy night many years ago, an elderly man and his wife entered the lobby of a small hotel in Philadelphia. The man helped his wife to a chair, then went to the desk. "All the big hotels in town are filled. Could you give me a room here?"

The clerk explained that there were three conventions in town and no rooms to be had anywhere. "Still, I can't send a nice couple like you out in the rain at one o'clock in the morning. Would you, perhaps, sleep in my room?"

The man replied that he couldn't put the clerk out of his room, but the clerk insisted. "Don't worry about me; I'll make out just fine."

The next morning, as he paid his bill, the elderly man said to the clerk, "You're the kind of manager who should be the boss in the best hotel in the country. Maybe someday I'll build one for you."

The clerk looked at the man and his wife and smiled. The three had a good laugh over the man's joke. Then the clerk helped them with their bags to the street.

Two years passed, and the clerk had forgotten the incident when he received a letter from the elderly man. It recalled the night of the storm, and enclosed was a round-trip ticket to New York for the young man to pay them a visit.

When the clerk reached New York, the man led him to the corner of Fifth Avenue and Thirty-fourth Street and pointed to a great new building, a palace of reddish stone with watchtowers, like a fairyland castle thrusting up into the sky.

"That," said the older man, "is the hotel I've just built for you to manage."

"You must be joking," the young man said, not quite knowing whether to believe his host or not.

"I most assuredly am not joking," the older man said with a slight smile.

"Who . . . just who are you?"

"My name is William Waldorf Astor. We are naming the hotel the Waldorf-Astoria, and you are to be its first manager."

The young man's name was George C. Boldt. And that is the story of how his service led him to a great life of managing one of the world's greatest hotels.

Serving others not only pays off in greater career opportunities, but it works in every area of life. Without exception, the most successful businesses are those that practice Christ's principle of serving others.

Think about the places you like to do business. Aren't they where people treat you like you're somebody and go out of their way to serve you?

Serving others is the way to build a great home life. A happy home is where people will do anything to help each other and work together to get the job done. Only foolish pride and stubbornness keep us from being servants, one to another in our homes.

When a person's goal shifts from serving to being served, that person's life soon begins to lose greatness. The business begins to fall apart, the home begins to deteriorate, the church goes downhill.

There is a spiritual law written by God: What you give is what you get. What you give in service is what comes back to you in life. If you give kindness, it comes back. If you give respect, it comes back. If you give interest, it comes back. If you give friendship, it comes back.

> Truly great people never stop serving others.

Serve a Power Greater Than Yourself

The *Oregonian* newspaper told a story about Al Erickson of Tigard and how he serves a power greater than he is. Along with the story was his picture, arms around one of the Christmas trees that he sells, holding hands with a woman and praying a prayer of blessing for her and her family. Al is a Christmas-tree farmer in Tigard. Thirteen years ago he was down on his knees cutting a tree for a customer when the Lord gave him the idea to pray for her and ask God's blessing on her family at Christmastime. Erickson said the woman got so excited she almost hugged him to death.

Ever since then, he has been praying for his customers. He sells about four hundred trees a year. Erickson and his customers join hands around the tree they have chosen for a tailor-made blessing. Year after year the people come back and tell Al what a special Christmas they had. They say, "You did it." Al says, "No, the Lord did it. I was the channel."

> A heart made right with God
> will become a serving heart.

To become successful in serving others you need a power greater than you are. Without this power, we are too proud, too arrogant, and too know-it-all to really help other people. Being headstrong gets us into a lot of trouble. When we try to go it alone and do our own thing, we always end up short.

A woman and her husband had backpacked deep into the forest of majestic Mt. Hood. After pitching camp for the night, they started exploring the immediate area around their campsite. The woman went off on her own and, before she knew it, was lost. She soon became disoriented and frightened. She yelled, but she was too far away for her husband to hear. For three days and nights she wandered around, trying to find her way. Fortunately some Mt. Hood rangers rescued her. She said she had learned that she needed to be awfully careful about going off and doing her own thing. She really couldn't make it in the forest without help.

You can't make it in life without the help of God. You can't begin to be the kind of serving person you want to be without the power greater than you are. You are not going to have the characteristics to serve well unless you know who the Boss is. These characteristics are humility, teachability, and unselfishness. The greatest day of your life will be when you stop wrestling and start nestling, when you stop fighting and surrender. To do the great things in life that you could do, you've got to surrender your life to Jesus Christ.

The late Frank Laubach was a tremendous pioneer missionary and server of people. God mightily used his life. Countless millions learned to read and write and to know Jesus through his ministry. He once said that if you want to know how a human being can find his value, you need to look at the sprinkler head. A sprinkler head by itself is not worth much. Its worth and power to accomplish comes through being connected to the water supply. In other words, it finds its fulfillment by being an instrument for carrying the water that makes the grass grow, the flowers bloom, and the vegetables flourish.

> God wants to use your life to bless others.
> But first it's got to be connected
> to the higher power—God.

Serve to Your Fullest Potential

Someone has said love is like a game of tennis: The player who serves will seldom lose. Someone else has said, he profits most who serves the best.

What enormous joy there is in serving the Lord. In Psalms 126:5, 6 we read, "Those who sow in tears will reap with songs of joy. He who goes out weeping, carrying seed to sow, will return with songs of joy, carrying sheaves with him."

There are five things you can do to serve to your potential.

Discover your potential   Discovery always comes in an encouraging environment. One thing the church should provide is a positive and uplifting environment in which people are discovering their potential. God created you with talents. The moment you receive Jesus as your Lord and Savior, you are given spiritual gifts. Do something that you enjoy. Don't be afraid to try new things. One of the ways you discover your potential is by doing things.

Dedicate your potential to God's glory   In this world there are three kinds of people. There are the drifters who drift through life doing nothing. There are the dropouts who give up before they get there. And there are the dedicated. God uses the dedicated person. You can be that dedicated person God uses. Ephesians 6:7 tells us to serve wholeheartedly. That means you put your heart and soul into it. You stop holding back and give yourself completely to serving.

Stretch to success.

Develop your potential God's gift to you is your potential. What you do with it is your gift back to God. Never limit your potential. Don't sell yourself short. Keep learning, keep improving. Michelangelo painted his greatest work when he was eighty years of age. It is never too early to start developing your potential. Today thirteen-year-old girls break world swimming records.

Use it or lose it.

Direct your potential Direct your life toward doing what you can do best. Be selective, be smart. I want to make my one life count as much as possible. I've seen people waste their lives doing things that didn't matter. If we're not careful, we spend all of our time on the urgent and leave out what's important. What really counts for now and eternity? How can I best serve the Lord?

Serve smart, not dumb.

Last September I was flying from Portland to the Midwest to speak at my old alma mater, Olivet University in Kankakee, Illinois. The man sitting by me was a national motivational speaker. We had a great time visiting back and forth and swapping a few stories and jokes.

He told me this story. A missionary had been sent into the jungles of Peru to do missionary work. He had dedicated his life to service of God and others. One day he was down by the river where the current was very strong, when he heard the cry of a native about to drown in the rapids. He took his clothes off, swam out, caught the man just in time, and was able to pull him to the shore.

No sooner had he gotten to the shore than another native came down the rapids crying to be saved. The missionary dived in again and saved the second man. This happened a third time, fourth time, fifth time.

The missionary was really getting exhausted by the time the sixth one appeared. He dived in and saved him. Barely making it back, he collapsed on the shore, so fatigued he could hardly move.

Here comes another one! This time the missionary can't move. All of his energy is spent. The man floats on by to his death. Then another one floats by, and the bodies keep coming down the river and floating to their death. The missionary is unable to do anything. He is absolutely spent. He has saved six lives. That's good, but could he have done better? Can you fault him? He gave everything he had. What do you think?

The missionary could have done better. He could have saved all of the natives if only he had walked up the bank of the river and stopped the wicked man who was throwing them into the river.

With such enormous needs all around us, with people drowning in hopelessness, despair, and broken relationships, we've got to put our energies where they count the most. We must not only work hard for Jesus, but work smart.

Working smart means working together. It is foolish for pastors to try to do the work of ministry by themselves. God's plan is for His people to work as a team, doing the work of ministry.

Do it now! Jesus said, "I must work the works of him that sent me, while it is day: the night cometh, when no man can work" (John 9:4 KJV).

Paul calls us to the same urgency of spirit: "Never be lazy in your work but serve the Lord enthusiastically" (Romans 12:11 TLB).

The way to serve to your fullest potential is to serve the Lord with enthusiasm—*now.* Do what is right in front of your nose.

NINETEEN
The Victory Principle

"... Greater is he that is in you, than he that is in the world" (1 John 4:4 KJV)

When Dwight D. Eisenhower was being inaugurated president of the United States in January, 1953, he surprised the nation by personally offering up a prayer to Almighty God. Here was a man who had commanded three million troops in the invasion of Normandy, had brought an end to World War II, and now was being inaugurated into the most powerful office in the world. And what did he do in front of all the nations of the world and all the people in America? He acknowledged that he needed help. He needed a Power greater than he was to fulfill the task before him.

Ike, when asked about this, said, "To the best of my knowledge, the men of courage I have known have been men of faith. I've never seen any of them who weren't."

In this chapter I have a very special word for anyone who is feeling defeated. I am going to share a principle that can help you not only face anything and everything but actually overcome it.

What is it that defeats a person? Family reverses? Yes. Financial setbacks? Yes. The loss of a loved one? Yes. Persecution or misunderstanding from other people? Yes. Negative attitudes? Yes. These things and many others cause us to become defeated.

But with this prime-time principle you need never be defeated.

The Apostle Paul had the victory principle operating in his life. Paul revealed that he had gone through tribulation, distress, persecution, all kinds of setbacks and harsh treatment. Yet, he could say ". . . in all these things we are more than conquerors through him who loved us" (Romans 8:37). Paul had discovered the victory that overcomes anything and everything.

To have a victory that overcomes anything and everything, you must have it on the inside. What is going on outside does not determine whether you live in victory or defeat; what is on the inside does.

Because of our need to have victory on the inside, Paul prays this prayer for us: "I pray that out of his glorious riches he may strengthen you with power through his Spirit in your inner being" (Ephesians 3:16).

A high school athlete with a lot of talent and promise was stricken with a disease that crippled his legs. He was living in total defeat because of this. After about a year of rehabilitation, he could walk with braces. But the worst problem was that he had defeat in his head. He had given up on life. He was powerless to do anything to help himself. You might say he had lost all hope.

Some friends took him to a very loving church. They had an open altar where they invited people in the service to come for prayer. A friend with the boy suggested that he go down and pray. He thought, *Well, I don't have anything to lose.* So he hobbled down the aisle with his braces . . . thump, thump, thump. He didn't really think it would do any good, but he decided he would go just to make his friend happy.

There at the place of prayer, people prayed for the healing of his body, mind, and spirit, that he would be touched by a Power greater than he was, that God would infuse him and impart His strength to him.

Something happened there that day to change the boy's life forever. It was not so much that his legs were healed. Years later he still walks with a severe limp. But what happened that day was greater than the healing of his legs. His mind was healed. As he touched God in faith and God touched him, the braces were taken off his mind. He was set free to believe that he could do something worthwhile with his life. With God's help, he could turn this setback into victory. He got up from there and went out and made something worthwhile out of his life. Today he is the president of one of the great colleges of America.

Are you ready for the victory principle?

> ". . . Greater is he that is in you, than he that is in the world" (1 John 4:4 kjv).

Without a Power Greater Than Yourself, You Are Not Going to Win

One of the greatest lessons you can ever learn is that in your own strength, you can't do it. In fact, to think you can is the pride that goes before a fall.

There are four good reasons why you need help beyond yourself.

To win the spiritual battle you are in, you've got to have a power greater than yourself You operate on four levels: the physical level, the intellectual level, the emotional level, and the spiritual level. The spiritual level deeply affects all other areas of your life. It is here that the battle rages over what kind of person you are going to be—healthy, whole, and happy or broken, unhappy, and self-destructive.

When you win the spiritual battle, it brings health and wholeness to your whole person. Ephesians 6:10–20 is a description of this spiritual battle. Paul writes, "Finally, be strong in the Lord and in his mighty power. Put on the full armor of God so that you can take your stand against the devil's schemes" (vv. 10, 11).

The creators of "Star Wars" recognized this eternal battle between the forces of good and evil. In *Return of the Jedi* there is a battle between Luke Skywalker and his father, Darth Vader, who has been taken over by the dark side. In that battle you see Luke, with all the good that is in him as a Jedi, fighting against the force of evil. The combat on the outside is fierce, but the struggle inside Luke is the real battle.

There is a fight between good and evil within him. If he allows his spirit to be taken over by hate, he will lose and be controlled by the dark side. But there he is, fighting against the forces of evil that know no mercy or justice, that only seek to win and destroy at all costs. You better believe there are destructive forces at work in our world and in our lives.

When *Return of the Jedi* was shown, some audiences broke out in cheers as Luke came out victorious in his struggle over the dark side. In doing so, he was able to defeat the evil spirit within his own father, Darth Vader, and restore him to the side of right before he departed into eternity. The story has a happy ending.

The reality is that no person, not even one like Luke Skywalker, can win the spiritual battle by himself. We need a power greater than we are to give us the edge that leads to victory.

Wake up! You are in a battle for your spiritual life. There are three spirits: God's Spirit, the human spirit, and the demonic spirit. The human spirit was created to be filled with another spirit. The human spirit is not going to remain in a vacuum. Either God's Spirit or the evil spirit will finally possess the human spirit.

Get it straight. The devil is your enemy. He is out to defeat you. The only way you can win this important battle is with a power greater than you. That power is God's power.

To keep positive and healthy in your outlook, you need a power greater than yourself   Let's face it! We live in a world surrounded by negatives. Isn't it odd that people who live in a land of abundance with so many opportunities can become so possessed with the negative?

Perhaps you have been having trouble keeping up in a down world. You try to think positive, but you keep getting pulled down into the negative. Instead of seeing what's right and what is possible, you keep seeing what's wrong and why it can't be done. You need help.

A Power greater than you are can help you. You can be ". . . transformed by the renewing of your mind" (Romans 12:2).

To do "greater things than these" you need a power greater than yourself   The older I become, the more I recognize that the important things I want to accomplish in my life cannot be done in my own human strength. There is no way I can fulfill the visions and dreams that God has given me by myself. From time to time the Holy Spirit reminds me of these words spoken by the Old Testament prophet Zechariah, ". . . 'Not by might nor by power, but by my Spirit,' says the Lord Almighty" (Zechariah 4:6).

> **Attempt great things for God**
> **and let God help you achieve them.**

To love other people the way you need to love them, you need a Power greater than yourself We live in a world of throwaway people. If somebody does not please us, we throw him or her away. If people don't live the way we think they should live, we discard them. We find out that someone we are relating to has faults and we discard that person.

God's love is so powerful that it never fails, never quits, and never gives up. This kind of love will hold us together in a family when all else fails. This kind of love will go the extra mile when others have given up. This kind of love will love in spite of the other person's failures and faults.

Meet the One Who Is Greater Than Yourself

> **Jesus is our Victor.**

Jesus Christ, the Son of God, came into our world of sin and suffering and setbacks. He came into our world of defeats. He faced everything that has ever defeated people. He was falsely accused and nailed to a cross. He shed great drops of blood. He died of a broken heart. On the third day the power of God raised Him from the dead, victorious. He is alive. He is our Victor.

Jesus said, ". . . In this world you will have trouble. But take heart! I have overcome the world" (John 16:33).

The spirit of Christ is given to us through the Holy Spirit.

When Jesus was to leave this earth and ascend back to the Father, He made it crystal clear that He was sending the Holy Spirit. Through the Holy Spirit, He would be with us. The spirit of victory and power would be ours through the Holy Spirit, who would not only be with us but live in us.

The big question is, have you received the Holy Spirit in your life? Jesus made it clear that we could not live the Christian life without the Holy Spirit. We could not be effective in our service without the Holy Spirit. We could not have that inner strengthening to overcome without the Holy Spirit. We could not love God's way without the Holy Spirit. We could not do great things for God without the Holy Spirit.

Tap Directly Into the Power

To tap into the power that will give you victory in your daily life, do these five things.

Receive Jesus as your Lord and Savior   At fifteen years of age, I invited Jesus Christ to come into my heart and take over the controls and direction of my life. Before that I was drifting, without any real purpose in life. Barely getting by in school and not getting along well with other people, I saw my life turn around the day I received Jesus Christ. He not only forgave my sins and gave me a new start, but gave me something worthwhile to live for.

Jesus is the connection
for worthwhile living.

On one occasion Jesus said, "I am the vine; you are the branches. . . . apart from me you can do nothing" (John 15:5). He also said at the same time, ". . . If a man remains in me and I in him, he will bear much fruit . . ." (John 15:5). Your life will have peace and joy and happiness and contentment. Your life will bless others. You will have a fruitful life. Basically Jesus is saying, "Connect with the vine, and everything will be fine."

Accept the fact that you are the temple of God   In ancient architecture, no building excelled the breathtaking splendor and beauty of the temple that Solomon built for God. It was magnificent. Only the holiest of priests would attempt to go into the inner sanctuary, because there the presence of God was so strong and overwhelming.

Where is the temple of God now? For years the ancient temple has lain in ruins. The Bible teaches us that the moment we receive Jesus Christ as our Lord and Savior, we become the temple of the Living God. God, through His Holy Spirit, comes to dwell and live within us.

The temple of God—that's you!

Through the Holy Spirit that lives within you, you have all the power and resources of God available to you to win victory.

Feed your mind on the Word of God   If you feed your mind on the soaps, the movies, what negative people say and do, you are going to live in defeat. Garbage in, garbage out. To have victory in your life, feed your mind on the Word of God.

The Bible says that faith comes by hearing and hearing by the Word of God. What this means is that as you daily read the Word of God, faith is built within you. A reservoir of victory lies within your thoughts, mind, and soul. As you have need of that, the Holy Spirit will recall it to you.

Meet God daily in prayer   You can't know God without spending time with Him. You can't have God's direction and power in your life unless you talk with Him in prayer.

Ephesians 6:18 tells us how to win, how to have victory, how to be on top. "And pray in the Spirit on all occasions with all kinds of prayers and requests. . . ."

> A person who daily spends time with the
> Lord in prayer cannot be defeated.

You say you don't have time to pray? My friend, prayer does not take time, it saves time. The days I spend time in extended prayer, I have energy, power, and a victory that I don't have any other way.

In Matthew 21:22 (KJV) we read, "And all things, whatsoever ye shall ask in prayer, believing, ye shall receive." The key word, the word that leads to victory, is that word *believing.* How do you overcome impossible things? By believing. By getting hooked up with a Power greater than you are. How do you do that? You do that through prayer.

As you make prayer a priority in your life and meet God the first thing in the morning, you're going to receive boldness and assurance. You will have new confidence and strength to face whatever you need to face. You're going to live in victory instead of defeat.

Cooperate with the Holy Spirit who lives within you   In your daily life you're not just out there doing your own thing. Be in communication with and sensitive to the Holy Spirit, who lives within you. Don't quench the Spirit. Don't ignore Him. Don't resist Him. Don't disobey Him. Say, "Yes, Lord." Fully cooperate with the Holy Spirit in the appointments of your daily life. Let Him rule in your thoughts. Let Him rule in the way you relate to other people. What an exciting way to live, letting Jesus live His life through you!

When people start cooperating with the Holy Spirit, ordinary living is turned into extraordinary living. Defeating habits are broken. Defeating life-styles are changed. Relationships begin to straighten out. New horizons open up.

My friend, you don't need to live with inferior feelings. You don't need to live bogged down by sin. You don't need to live in defeat, because where you are weak, He is strong. Where you don't have it, He has it. Get up and live by this victory principle: ". . . Greater is he that is in you, than he that is in the world" (1 John 4:4 KJV).